A Singer's Guide to the Larynx

ANATOMY WITH IMAGINATION
A Singer's Guide to the Larynx

Nicola Harrison and Alan Watson

Compton Publishing
This edition first published 2020 © 2020 by Compton Publishing Ltd.

Registered office: Compton Publishing Ltd, 30 St. Giles', Oxford, OX1 3LE, UK
Registered company number: 07831037

Editorial offices: 35 East Street, Braunton, EX33 2EA, UK
Web: www.comptonpublishing.co.uk

The right of the authors to be identified as the authors of this work has been asserted in accordance with the UK Copyright, Designs and Patents Act 1988.

All rights reserved. No part of this publication may be reproduced, stored in a retrieval system, or transmitted, in any form or by any means, electronic, mechanical, photocopying, recording or otherwise, except as permitted by the UK Copyright, Designs and Patents Act 1988, without the prior permission of the publisher.

Trademarks: Designations used by companies to distinguish their products are often claimed as trademarks. Any brand names and product names used in this book are trade names, service marks, trademarks or registered trademarks of their respective owners. The publisher is not associated with any product or vendor mentioned in this book.

Disclaimer: This book is designed to provide helpful information on the subject discussed. This book is not meant to be used, nor should it be used, to diagnose or treat any medical condition. For diagnosis or treatment of any medical condition, consult your own physician. The publisher and author are not responsible for any specific medical condition that may require medical supervision and are not liable for any damages or negative consequences to any person reading or following the information in this book. References are provided for informational purposes only and do not constitute endorsement of any product, website, or other source.

Permissions: Where necessary, the publisher and author(s) have made every attempt to contact copyright owners and clear permissions for copyrighted materials. In the event that this has not been possible, the publisher invites the copyright owner to contact them so that the necessary acknowledgments can be made.

ISBN 978-1-909082-58-8
A catalogue record for this book is available from the British Library.

Cover design: Louise Hill, http://www.louise-hill.com
and David Siddall, http://www.davidsiddall.com

Set in 14pt Cambria by Kerrypress Ltd, St Albans
Printed in the UK and USA

1 2020

Contents

Section I The larynx: basic anatomy   **1**
    Overview   **3**
    Position   3
    Cartilages   5
    Membranes   5
    Muscles   5
    Function   7
    Individual parts
    Epiglottis   9
    Thyroid cartilage   11
    Vocal folds   13
    Cricoid cartilage   15
    Arytenoid cartilages   17
    Tracheal rings   21
    Nerve supply   **23**
    Questionnaires, games and worksheets   **24**

Section II The muscles of the Larynx   **33**
    Overview: Intrinsic muscles of the Larynx   **35**
        i)   Cricothyroid muscles   37
        ii)   Cricoarytenoid muscles: posterior and lateral   39
        iii)   Interarytenoid muscles   43
        iv)   Aryepiglottic muscles   45
        v)   Thyroarytenoid muscles   47
    Overview: Extrinsic muscles of the larynx   **51**
    Direct extrinsic muscles
        i)   Thyrohyoid muscles   51
        ii)   Sternothyroid muscles   52

Indirect extrinsic muscles			**52**
	i)	Sternohyoid muscles	52
	ii)	Omohyoid muscles	52
Other extrinsic muscles			**55**
	i)	Stylohyoid Muscles	55
	ii)	Digastric muscles	55
	iii)	Geniohyoid muscles	55
	iv)	Hyoglossus muscles	55
	v)	Mylohyoid muscles	56
	vi)	Pharyngeal constrictors	56
Questionnaires, games and worksheets			**57**

Section III: The vocal folds — 63
Overview
Vocal folds — 65
Vocal ligaments — 67
False vocal folds and ventricles — 69
Vocal fold cycle — 70
Mucosal wave — 71
Questionnaires, games and worksheets — **72**

Section IV: Putting it all together — 79
Introduction — 81
Overview — 83
Internal shape and structures — 85
Epithelium & Reinke's space — 90
The creation of sound — 93
Aspects of sound — 94
Pitch — 94
Harmonics — 101

Types of phonation in singing	**102**
Vocal qualities	104
Timbre	106
Registers	107
Vibrato	110
Questionnaires, games and worksheets	**112**
About the Authors	**119**

Dedication

I will sing with my spirit, but I will also sing with my understanding.
1 Corinthians 14:15.

Copyright notice

Customers may photocopy outline images for colouring, quizzes and tests for own use. All other text and images are subject to copyright law and may not be photocopied or reproduced in any format without permission.

Instructors adopting the book may apply for permissions to reproduce images for classroom use.

Acknowledgements

Particular thanks to Johan Sundberg, Jeanie LoVetri, Gillyanne Kayes and Kerry Obert for offering a variety of suggestions and viewpoints particularly in regard to Section IV where Alan and I make a valiant attempt to nail some cautious definitions to the mast of contention.

Thanks as always to Noel at Compton for his easy-going nature and free rein; To Alan for his forbearance when our singer-scientist discussions became volatile; To Johan and Gillyanne for kindly providing quotes and Foreword. To Louise Hill for cover design and her additional artwork and to our wonderful profession of singing for all the curiosity, joy and endless wonder it has provided me with over so many years. I hope this book shines a light for all those seeking to understand the anatomy of the larynx and how it works.

Finally, thank you for buying this book.

Nicola Harrison

Foreword

Singing teaching has long been a rather competitive profession. In the 21st century the social media conversations and the power of the web provide a handy forum for those who promote themselves as experts in voice, often with minimal knowledge and experience.

The study of voice is multi-faceted and can include the disciplines of medicine, acoustics, psychology and neuroscience as well as the more obvious skills of musical interpretation and performance communication. Between them, the authors are able to cover a number of these areas, having qualifications in neuroscience, anatomy and physiology, psychology of performance, nursing, musical performance and text.

What Nicola Harrison and Alan Watson have set out to do here is to provide a digestible and straightforward guide to the nuts and bolts of vocal anatomy and physiology in relation to commonly used terms in vocal pedagogy. Perhaps it will act as a litmus test for those swimming in a tide of loudly paraded opinions, to help sort the wheat from the chaff and inspire its readers to have the courage to find out more for themselves.

Dr Gillyanne Kayes

Introduction

The vocal instrument is an extraordinary, complicated mechanism that lies hidden within us. It is made up of many different parts and is supported and maintained by so many muscles, joints and cartilages, that its anatomy and function in relation to the act of singing has often been veiled in mystery.

This workbook has been written specifically for singers, students and teachers of singing and has a strong imaginative and pictorial element to help visualise the internal workings of one key part of that instrument: the larynx. Offered as a manual for teachers to work with and share with their students, we hope that the beautiful design and mixed approach to learning will help the reader engage with this complex subject in an interesting way.

In writing this book we have offered up multiple diagrams and views. These are all original work and have been created by the authors specifically for *The Singer's Guide to the Larynx*. We have used a consistent colour scheme for the cartilages, so that the full structure and function of the larynx can be clearly grasped. This is accompanied by concise and scientifically accurate text based on current understanding and, where knowledge is incomplete, we have endeavoured to make that clear.

In the past, some anatomical terms have been used loosely in both scientific and vocal literature which may have led to confusion. We have attempted to clarify this by using the same terms consistently throughout the book. We have given alternative terms in brackets so that readers can see that they are one and the same thing.

Our descriptions here are limited to the larynx only and do not set out to describe the anatomy of the entire vocal instrument, or the different systems that support it. We hope to address this in further volumes.

The larynx is hard to picture from within. We have therefore done our best to produce clear and accurate descriptions of this mechanism in order to lay bare its component parts and show how they work together to produce sound. We have also added some playful images to the first section to help learners associate anatomical structures with known shapes.

Combining anatomy with colourful figures will, we hope, help young singers picture their instrument in a variety of ways. To this end, the book is also supported by imaginative learning games to tease the mind and test knowledge. The questionnaires make fantastic tools for teachers who wish to check their students' knowledge and review their own learning.

As each section develops from the previous one, an element of repetition is used to build on information previously given to gradually extend learning. In the final section, we valiantly attempt to put the previous sections together in terms of physiology and explain the most contentious areas of our profession as best we can. Sometimes, in the absence of hard evidence, this can be tough.

By bringing the wonderful resource of imagination to the teaching of vocal anatomy, we hope to provide singers at varying levels with a visually alluring and mentally stimulating approach to understanding the structure and function of the larynx.

Nicola Harrison and Alan Watson

Note on labelling of figures

We have used simple terms throughout to denote which views we are showing in the figures. These are mainly labelled as front, side and rear views. However, in a couple of figures we have offered other sections of the larynx:

Coronal section – a view of a slice that separates the front of a structure from the back.

Sagittal section – a view of a slice that separates one side of a structure from the other.

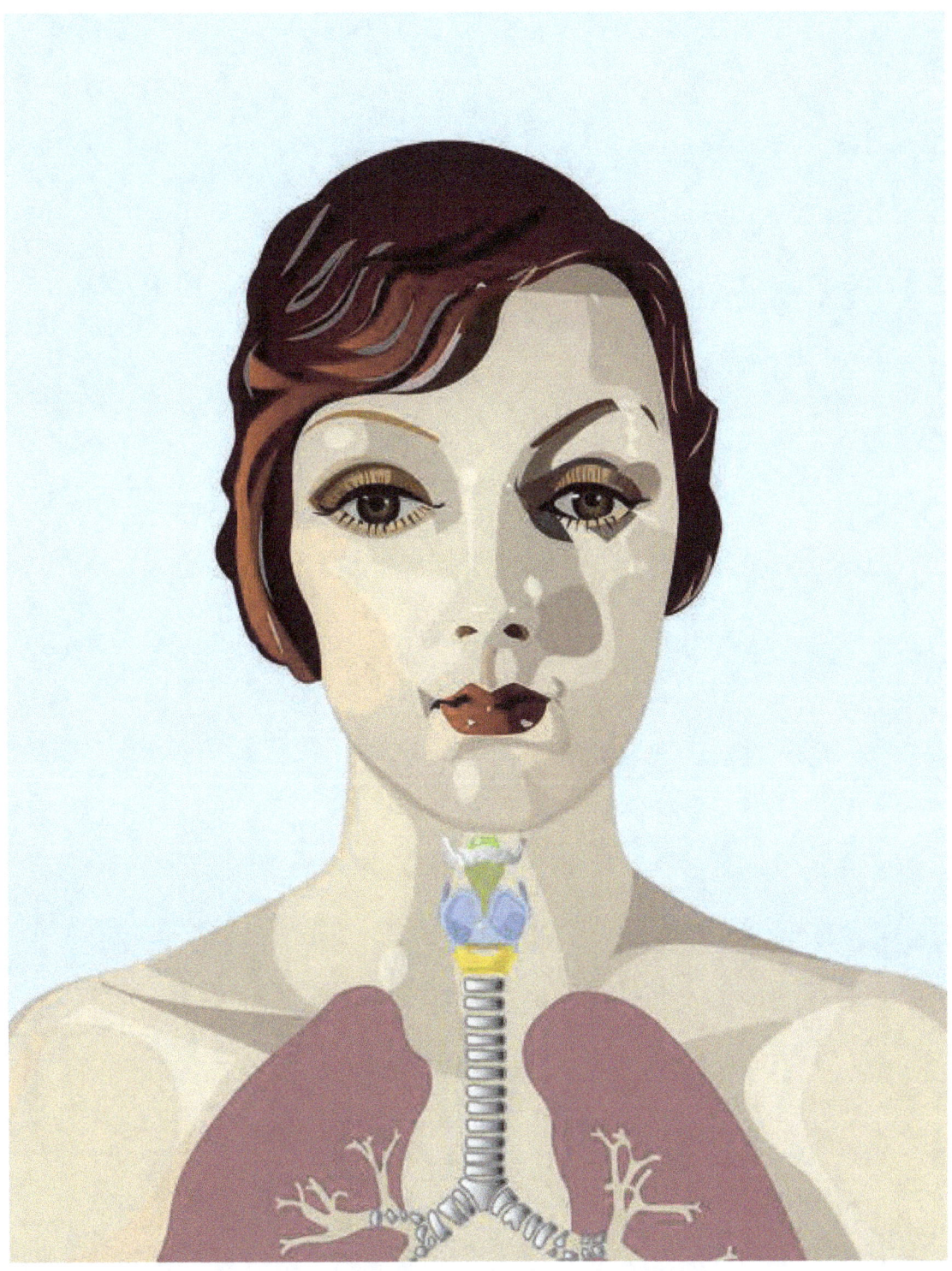

This beautiful image of a 1920s fashion mannequin shows the correct position of the larynx and trachea within the body.

Section I The larynx: basic anatomy

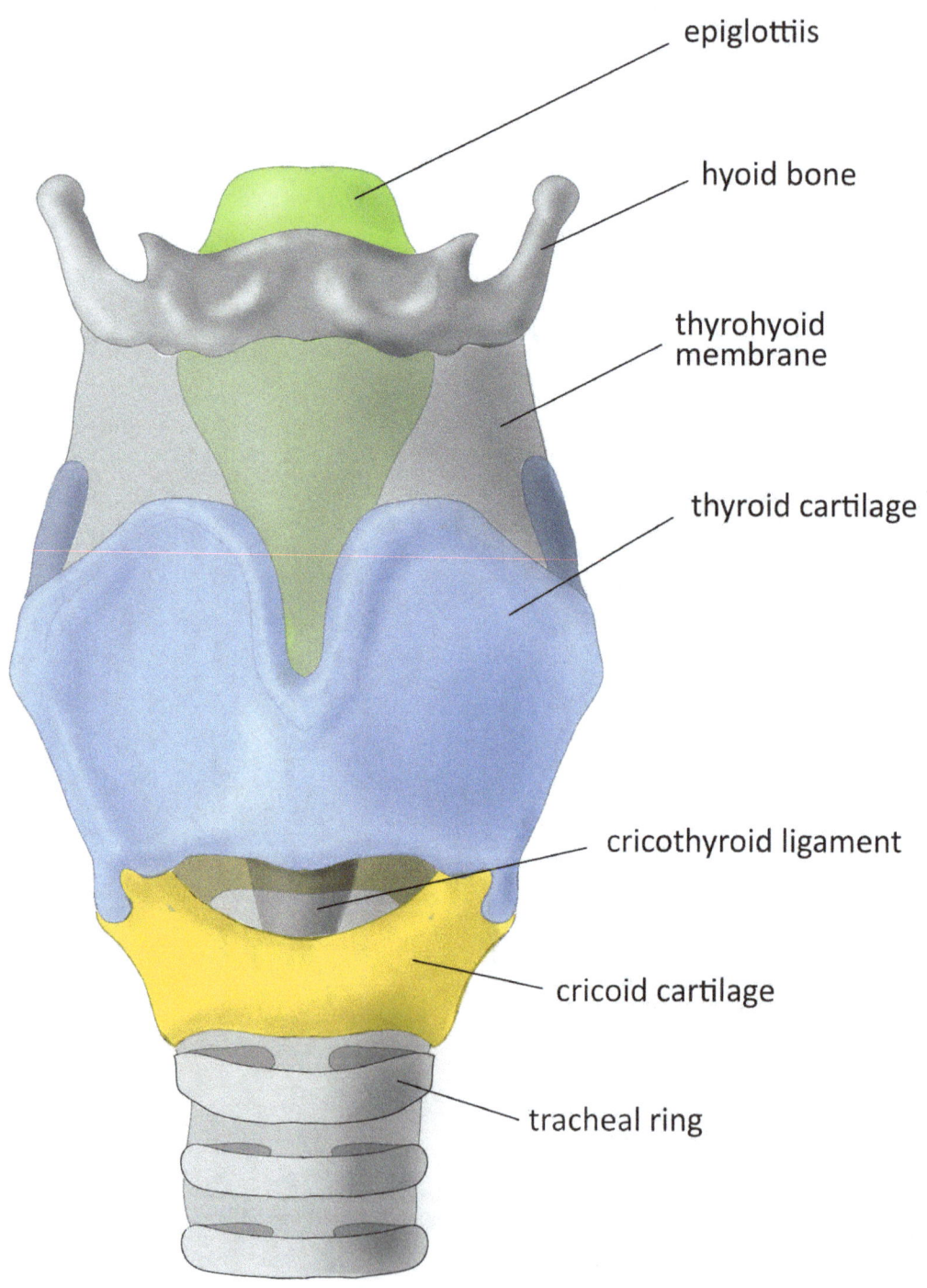

Front view of the larynx

Overview

Position

The larynx is located at the front of the neck and sits directly above the trachea or windpipe. In size, the larynx is around 3.6 cm in length in women and around 4.4 cm in men, although size may vary. It can be seen and felt as a prominent bump in adult males and felt as a firm structure within the neck of adult females. It is less prominent in children.

Behind it lies the oesophagus (food pipe) a flattened tube which sits in front of the cervical (neck) vertebrae.

The larynx is suspended from **the hyoid bone**. This is not part of the larynx but provides attachments for muscles to the tongue, larynx and skull. It sits above the trachea which is held open by a series of cartilaginous rings, known as the **tracheal rings**.

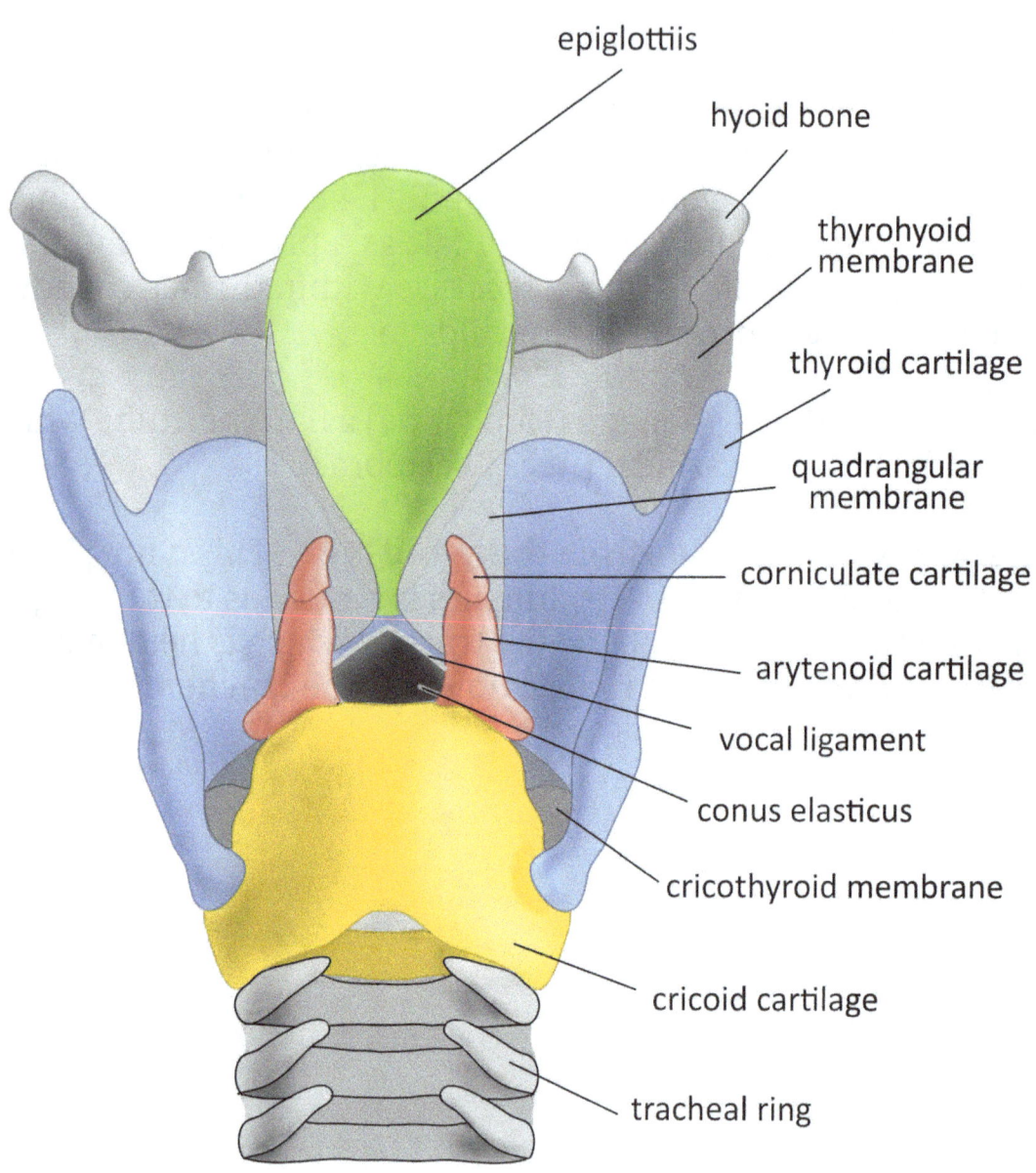

Rear view of the larynx

Description

Cartilages

The larynx is composed of three large cartilages. These are:

1. The **epiglottis**
2. The **thyroid cartilage**
3. The **cricoid cartilage**

It also contains some smaller cartilages. The most important of these are:

4. The **arytenoid cartilages**

Membranes

The large cartilages of the trachea and larynx are connected by membranes which allow some movement between them and form a continuous tube to contain the air. These are:

1. The **thyrohyoid membrane:** this runs from the upper surface and superior horns of the thyroid cartilage to the hyoid bone.

2. The **cricothyroid membrane**: this has two parts. The largest is the **conus elasticus**, a tent-like membrane which runs upwards from the upper edge of the cricoid cartilage to the vocal folds. The other part is the narrow **cricothyroid ligament** which runs from the front of the cricoid cartilage to the lower edge of the thyroid cartilage (see also Section II).

3. The **quadrangular membranes:** the upper edges of these run from the arytenoid cartilages to the epiglottis. The lower edge is continuous with the vestibular ligament of the false vocal folds the membranes between the **tracheal rings** that link them.

Muscles

Within the larynx there are a number of muscles that move the cartilages, open and close the vocal folds and are responsible for generating sound. These are called the **intrinsic muscles** of the larynx.

Outside the larynx, the **extrinsic muscles** are responsible for controlling its position in the neck.

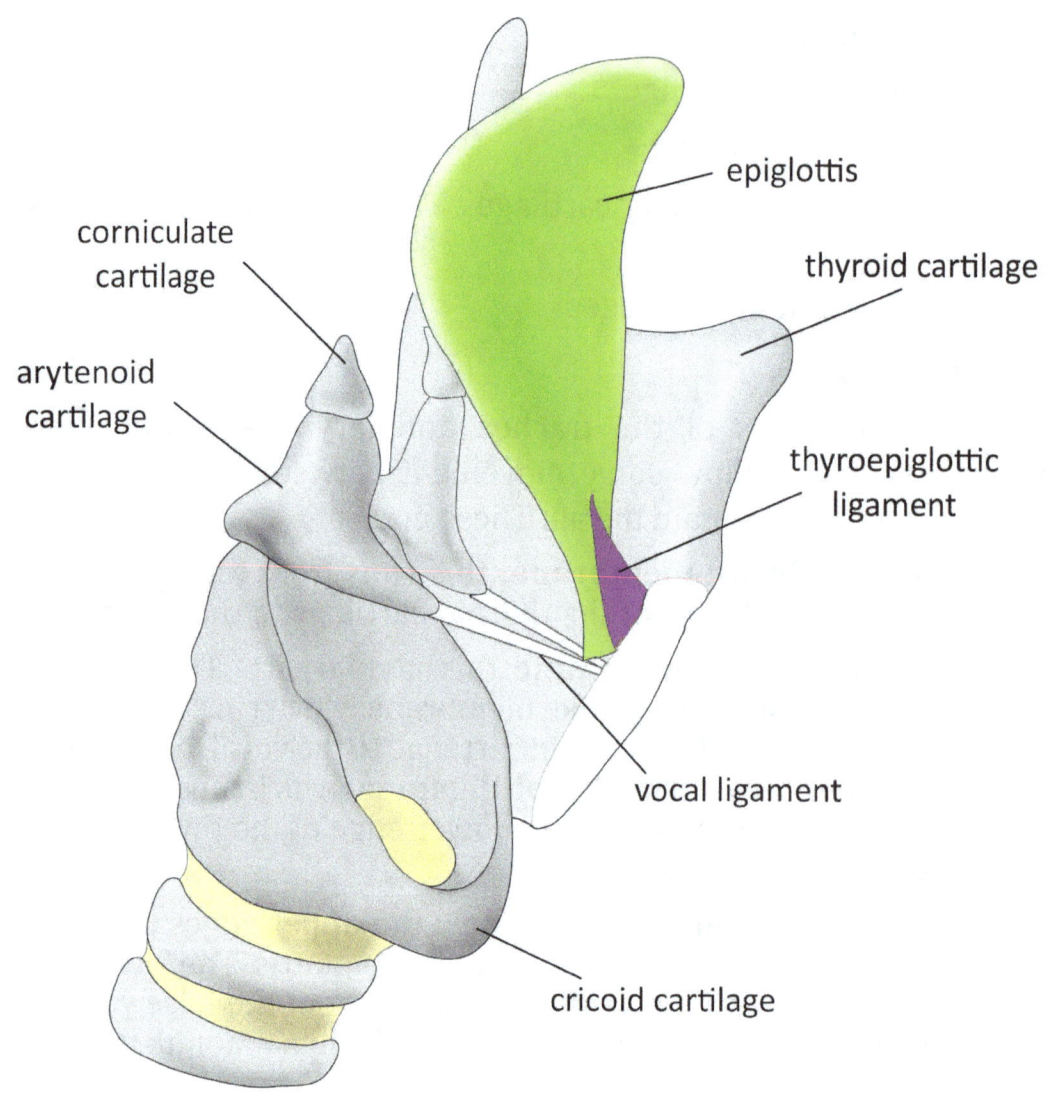

Attachment of the epiglottis from the side. Note that half of the thyroid cartilage has been removed to show the thyroepiglottic ligament

Function of the larynx

Although we now think of the larynx primarily as the organ of voice production, its original function was simply to prevent choking by closing off the trachea during swallowing. This closure was achieved through the action of two muscular flaps within the larynx, known as the **vocal folds.**

During evolution, the **epiglottis** developed to take over this function leaving the vocal folds free for phonation (speaking and singing).

Let us now review the individual components.

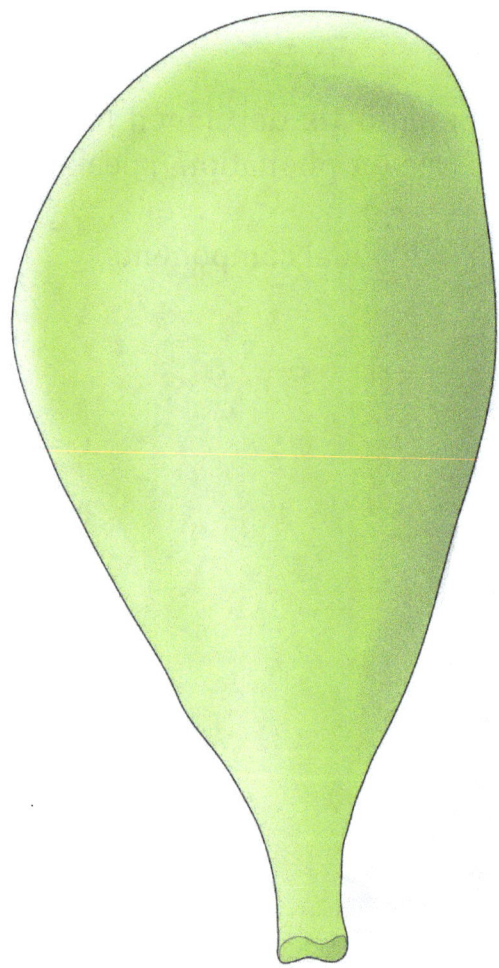

The epiglottis

The Epiglottis

Description

The epiglottis is a leaf-shaped structure that lies behind the tongue. The pointed end of the 'leaf' is attached to the front inner surface of the thyroid cartilage by the thyroepiglottic ligament.

Although flattened, the epiglottis has a slight curve to its surface.

Function

The epiglottis closes off the top of the larynx to prevent food, drink or foreign bodies getting into the airway.

During swallowing the larynx is pulled upwards by the extrinsic muscles (see Section II). At the same time as the larynx is being pulled upwards, the tongue moves backwards, pushing the epiglottis down to close off the upper opening of the larynx.

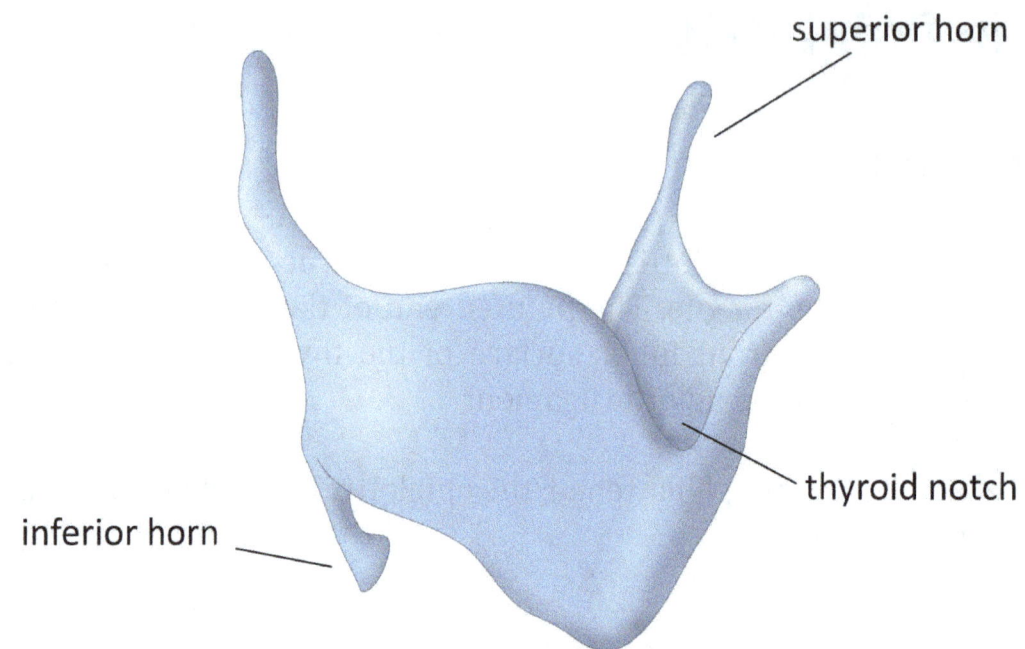

Front view of the thyroid cartilage

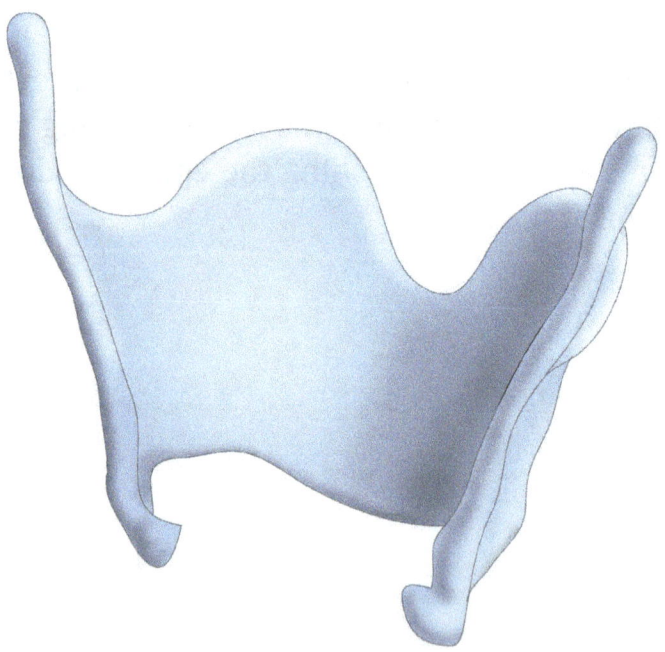

Rear view of the thyroid cartilage

The thyroid cartilage

Description

The **thyroid cartilage** is the largest cartilage in the larynx. It has a shield-like shape with a ridge at the front. It is larger in men and known as the *Adam's Apple*. It is tightly curved at the front and open at the back.

It has a pair of horns on each side, one pair of which points upwards and the other pair downwards. The upward-pointing horns are attached to the **thyrohyoid membrane.** The downward-pointing horns form a joint with the cricoid cartilage. This is called the **cricothyroid joint.**

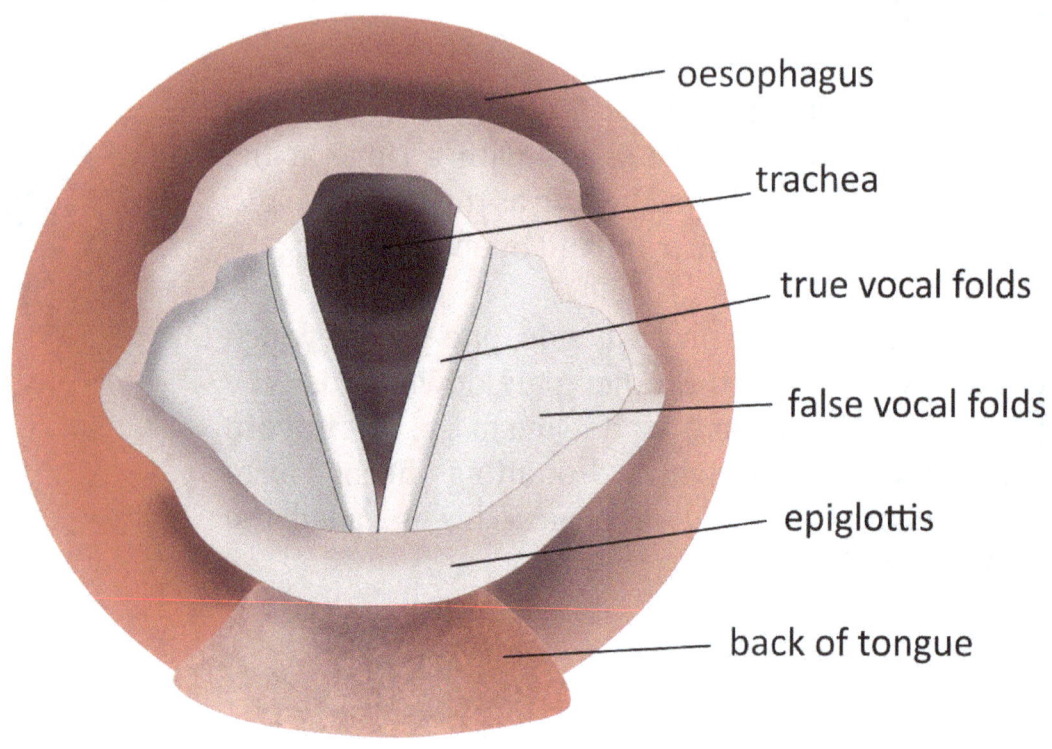

The vocal folds seen from above. Note: The entry to the larynx, where the vocal folds are situated, is behind and below the back of the tongue.

The Vocal Folds

Description

The true vocal folds are two horizontal muscular flaps that lie behind the thyroid cartilage. These folds are long and narrow.

They are attached, at one end, to the inner surface of the **thyroid cartilage**. At the other end, they are attached to the **arytenoid cartilages**. When air passes between them, the folds vibrate and generate sound.

The false vocal folds are far less involved in sound production and are discussed in Section III.

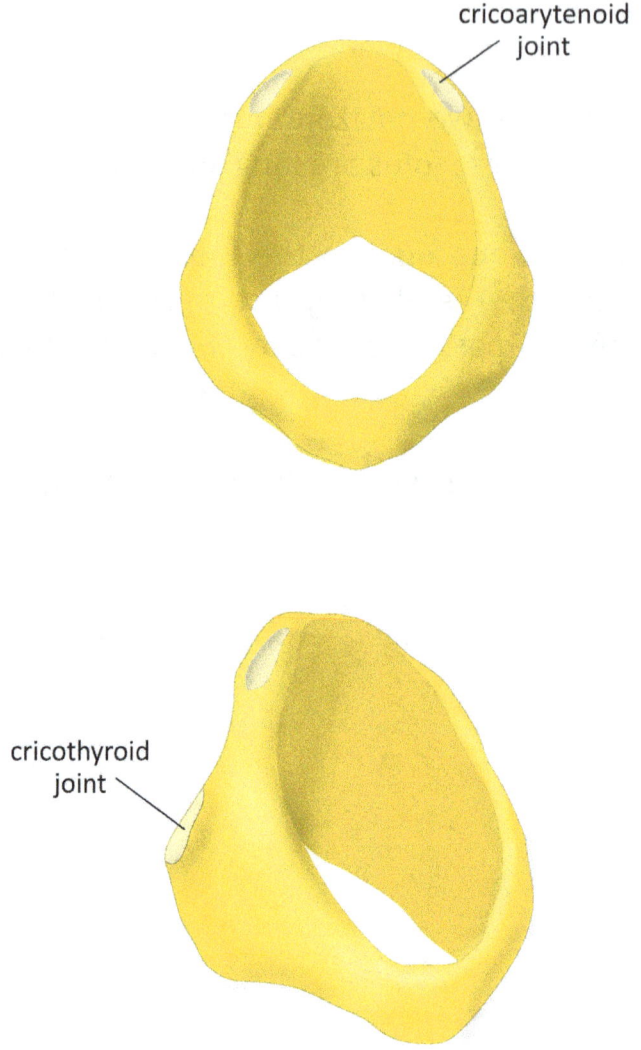

Front and side views of the cricoid cartilage

The cricoid cartilage

Description

Unlike the thyroid cartilage, which is open at the back, the **cricoid cartilage** completely encircles the airway. Situated directly below the thyroid cartilage, it is shaped like a signet ring with the 'seal' at the back.

On the upper surface of the 'seal' are situated the joints on which the two arytenoid cartilages are placed (the **cricoarytenoid joints**). These cartilages are attached to the rear end of the vocal folds. On the lower half of the 'seal' are the **cricothyroid joints**. These connect the **cricoid** and the **thyroid** cartilages.

Function

The cricoid cartilage provides a base for the arytenoid cartilages which in turn are attached to the vocal folds. *If* either the cricoid cartilage rotates backwards *or* the thyroid cartilage rotates downwards at the cricothyroid joint (the jury is still out on this), then the vocal folds will be stretched and the pitch of the voice will be raised (see further discussions in Sections III and IV. When the rotation at the cricothyroid joint is in the opposite direction, the vocal folds are slackened (i.e. the tension is reduced), lowering the pitch of the voice.

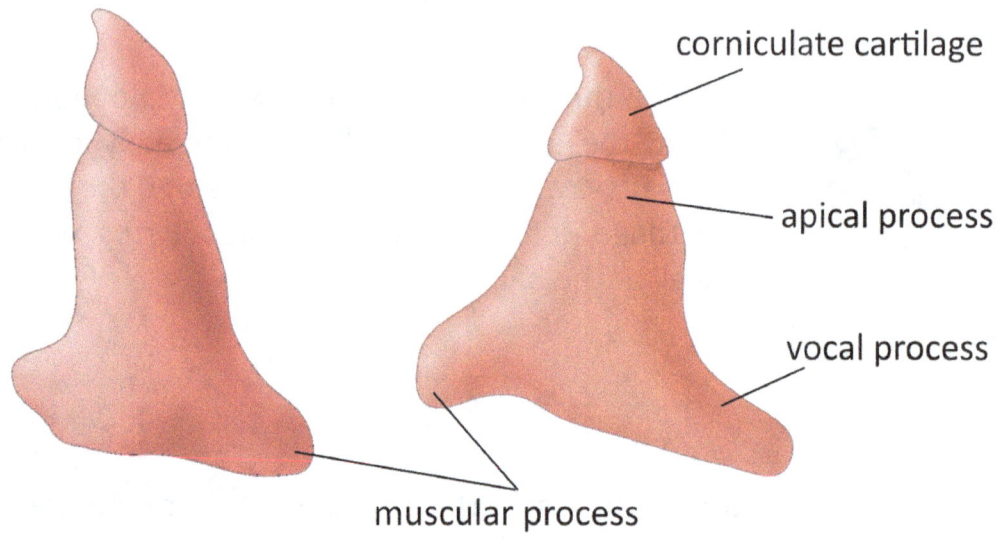

Rear and side views of the arytenoid cartilages

The arytenoid cartilages

Description

The two **arytenoid cartilages** are situated on the upper edge of the 'seal' part of the cricoid cartilage. Structurally, these are shaped like pyramids with three sides.

Each pyramid has three extensions arising from its corners. These elongations or *processes* are called:

>The **vocal process**
>The **apical process**
>The **muscular process**

The **vocal process** points forwards and is attached to the vocal folds.

The **muscular process** points to the side and provides the attachment for the muscles that open and close the vocal folds.

The **apical process** points upwards and supports the small **corniculate cartilage** which sits on top of it like a hat. From this apical process, arises a sheet of tissue that connects it with the epiglottis and is called the **aryepiglottic fold**.

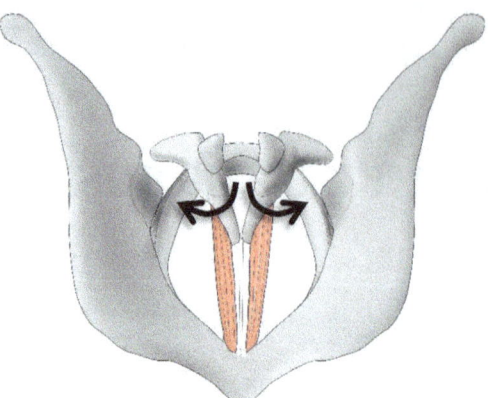

Figure 1. Movement of the arytenoid cartilages. Viewed from above, demonstrating lateral, or sideways rotation of the arytenoid cartilages. This opens the space between the vocal folds (glottis).

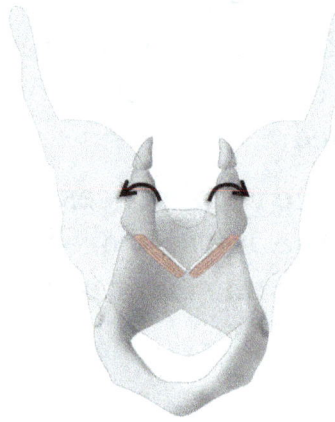

Figure 2. Frontal view of how outward-rolling movements of arytenoid cartilages tilt the apical processes sideways. This raises the free edges of the vocal folds.

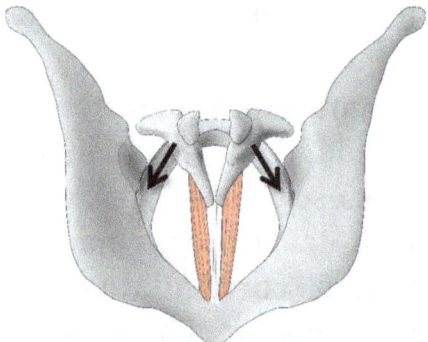

Figure 3. Seen from above to show forward sliding of the arytenoid cartilages. This may occur when the vocal folds are stretched in order to raise the pitch of the note sung.

Movement of the arytenoid cartilages

Function

The main function of the arytenoid cartilages is to open and close the space between the vocal folds. This is known as the glottis. The vocal folds move apart to open the glottis for breathing in. When making sound, the folds are brought together to close the glottis.

The joints between the arytenoid cartilages and the cricoid cartilage are called the cricoarytenoid joints. These allow the two arytenoid cartilages to rotate and slide.

There are two planes of rotation. The first is a lateral rotation allowing the vocal processes to turn outwards (Figure 1). The second plane of rotation is an outward-rolling movement which allows the apical processes to tilt sideways, lifting the free edge of the vocal folds. When they rotate in one direction, the vocal processes move apart. This opens the glottis.

When they move in the opposite direction, the vocal processes come together and the glottis closes (Figure 2).The joint also allows the arytenoid cartilages to slide backwards and forwards along the edge of the cricoid cartilage (Figure 3).

NOTE: Planes of rotation of the cricoarytenoid joints

Because movement of the vocal folds is normally assessed using a laryngoscope, it has not been possible to see small changes in depth. It is therefore difficult to fully differentiate between the exact contributions of the two planes of rotation, shown in Figures 1 and 2, to the movement of the vocal folds.

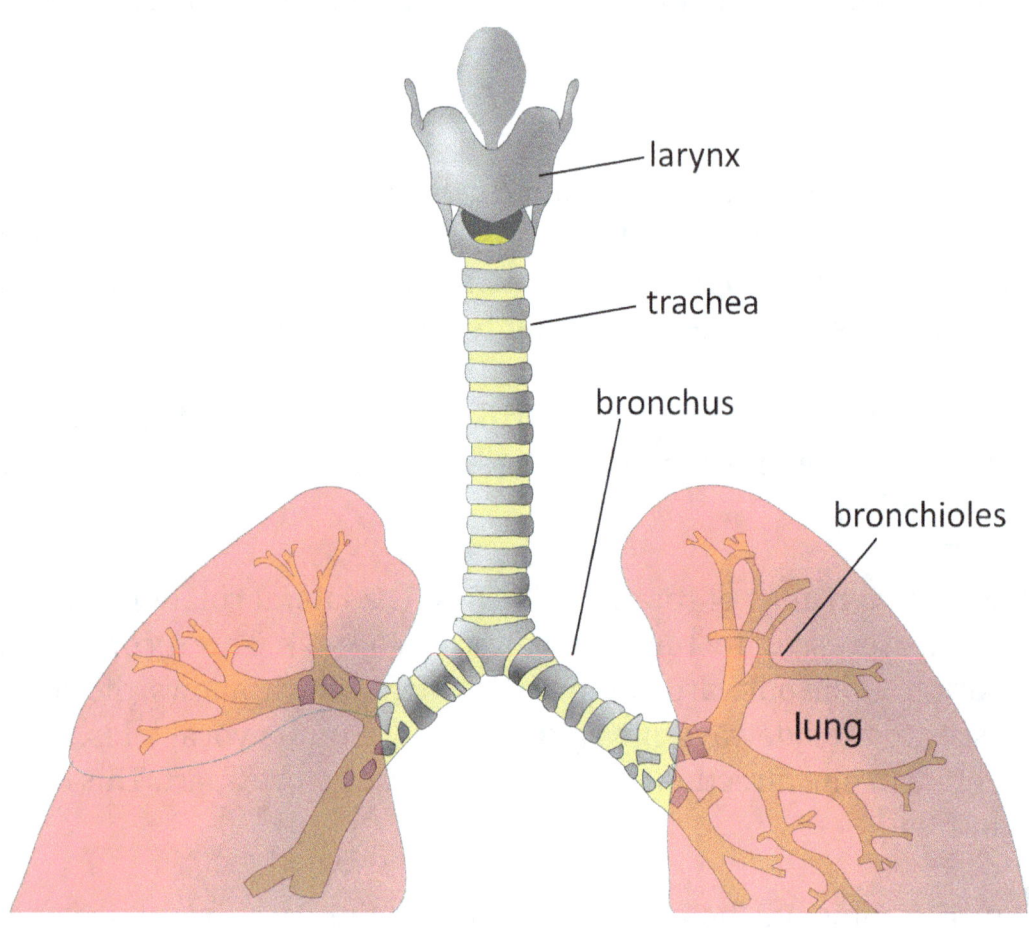

Front view of the tracheal rings and upper part of the lungs

The tracheal rings

Description

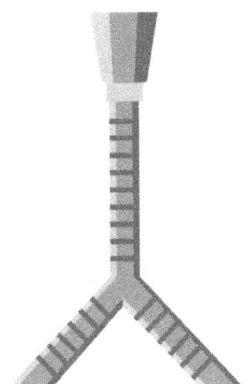

Although the trachea is technically outside the larynx, we have included it in this section because it arises from the larynx and is a continuation of it.

The tracheal rings continue from the base of the larynx to the lower end of the trachea which then branches into two bronchi, one of which enters each lung. These then branch further into various lobes within the lung.

Unlike the cricoid cartilage, the tracheal rings do not encircle the larynx completely and are open at the back.

They provide a rigid framework for the trachea and keep the tracheal space open for the passage of air to and from the lungs. This prevents the airway from collapsing. Viewed from the front, the trachea and bronchi look something like a shower hose.

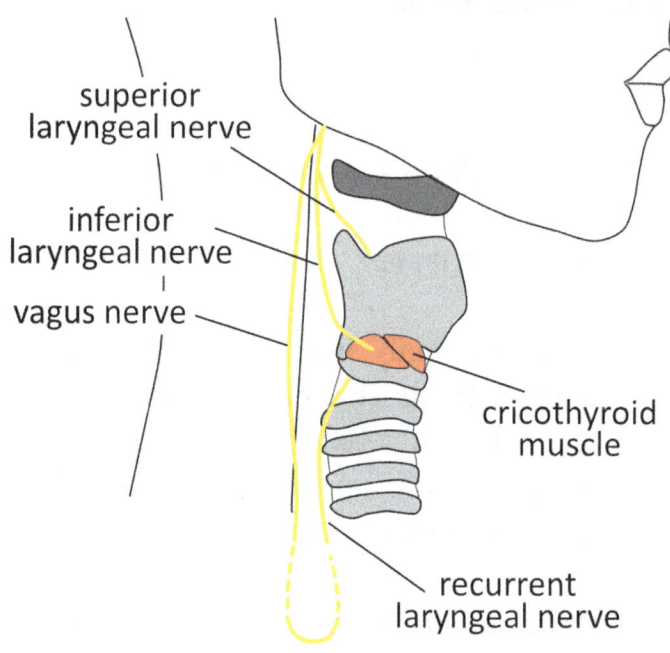

Nerve supply to the larynx - side view

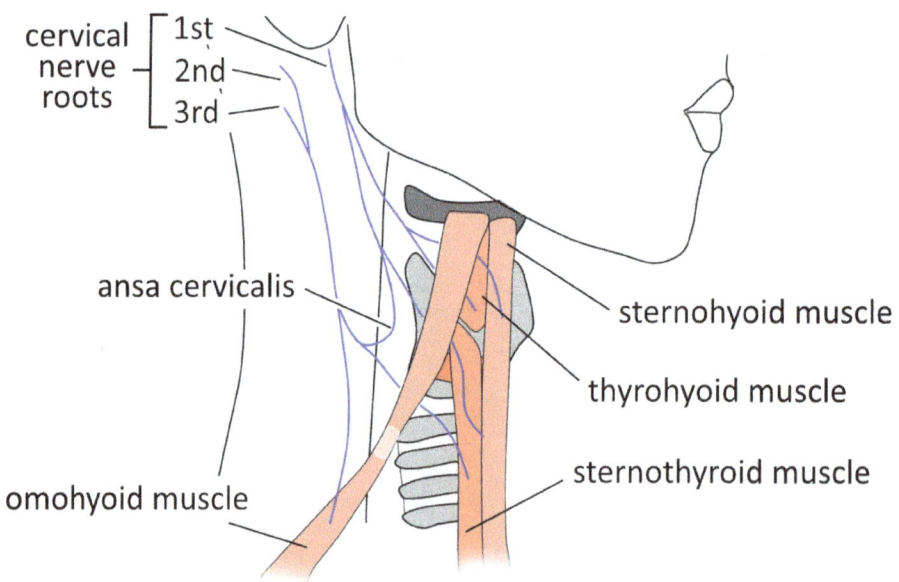

Nerve supply to extrinsic muscles of the larynx - side view

Nerve supply

The following paragraph summarises, as simply as possible, some basic information about the nerve supply to the larynx.

On each side, the larynx is supplied by the **vagus nerve**. This arises directly from the hind brain or **medulla oblongata** and has two branches running to the larynx. These are:

> The **superior laryngeal nerve**
> The **recurrent laryngeal nerve**

The superior laryngeal nerve branches to form **the external laryngeal nerve**, which controls the cricothyroid muscles, and **the internal laryngeal nerve**, which carries sensation from the region above the glottis. The recurrent laryngeal nerve controls all of the intrinsic muscles of the larynx, except for the cricothyroid muscles, and also carries sensation from below the vocal folds to the brain.

The extrinsic muscles that control the position of the larynx in the neck (the strap muscles) are supplied by nerves arising from the upper segments of the spinal cord in the neck. These are known as the **cervical roots 1–3.** Branches of these nerve roots form a loop. This is called the **ansa cervicalis.**

For more about laryngeal muscles please see Section II.

Revision questionnaire A

Section I: Cartilages and vocal folds

1. What are the main cartilages in the larynx?
2. Which of these is shaped like a signet ring?
3. Which of these is shaped like a leaf?
4. Which of these is shaped like a shield?
5. Which of these are shaped like a pyramid?
6. Where are the vocal folds located?
7. Where are the arytenoid cartilages located?
8. What are the attachments of the cricothyroid membrane?
9. Which ligament attaches it to the thyroid cartilage?
10. What is the nickname of the bump at the front of the thyroid cartilage?
11. How does movement at the cricothyroid joint affect the sound?

Revision questionnaire B

Section I Cartilages and Vocal Folds

1. What is the role of the epiglottis?
2. What was the original role of the vocal folds?
3. Which structure now has that function?
4. What shape does this structure resemble?
5. Describe the vocal folds.
6. What is the name of the space between the vocal folds?
7. Which cartilages are the vocal folds attached to, front and back?
8. What is the shape of the cricoid cartilage?
9. Where, on this shape, do the arytenoid cartilages sit?
10. What are the names of the three processes that form part of the arytenoid cartilages?
11. What is the main function of the arytenoid cartilages?

Word matching

Draw lines to pair the correct anatomical terms related to vocal folds and cartilages of the larynx.

Vocal	Ring
Thyroid	Adam's
Cartilage	Process
Process	Cricothyroid
Thyrohyoid	Ligament
Apical	Hyoid
Joint	Fold
Tracheal	Membrane
Apple	Vocal
Ariepiglottic	Arytenoid
Bone	Notch

Larynx wordsearch

```
E H C T L G B L X D M Q E S H E B Z K G I Q J T
D E X Q I L E L B V O C A L P R O C E S S K T M
X F S B I O A R I E P I G L O T T I C V C Q H N
Z Q S G Y G F G D O F V T I O P O K U T E Q Y Y
C S X U A T S K S I H P Y U P M R U M B K G R U
R Z R P E H F A D A M S A P P L E L U H B A O P
W E C R I C O I D T U K H I S Y S Z C J U N I Y
Q Z C R Q G A G W Z X X C V W M Z F O J M O D M
L Q N N Q T T G A R Y T E N O I D P S E Z W Z O
J T Z R H Y E A E T I D D W K S R L A U T J M E
U I G B U Z F J P R F L T P O E Y P Y F Z M H F
D F U X H E C S N A F L W X P I E Z Z V T A G J
Z I O Y V D Z K O C M E N C A R T I L A G E N E
O W A Z T G X M T H E D M W T U F I B T K W E N
N D V Q Z K V Y C E V U A L C L I O S O U T G C
U F Z Z G T G S H A D S F L G L H F A Y W N C M
W I M Z O L N L P Z O O P I T C H A P D E U O G
Y E U R M E W C Y N M E M B R A N E I J C X S E
M Q S N G L A R Y N X W W H P Z I T C F C R S M
O K C F I S R F K N G R C Z D P W A A K E G T E
Q Q W T C Y D I E T X X D P Q O I Y L Y V I G P
K P L W H J T S Z V S H Y O I D N F J H X J E O
N W K A T X M Z O M E Q L R Z L I Z Z F W E R G
B M H O N T F N D M W Q C R T T M T Y O X P H F
```

Larynx	Trachea	Aryepiglottic
Mucosa	Notch	Apical
Adam's apple	Cricoid	Cartilage
Thyroid	Pitch	Vocal process
Hyoid	Membrane	Arytenoid

Colouring anatomy of the larynx 1

Colour and label the separate parts of the diagram

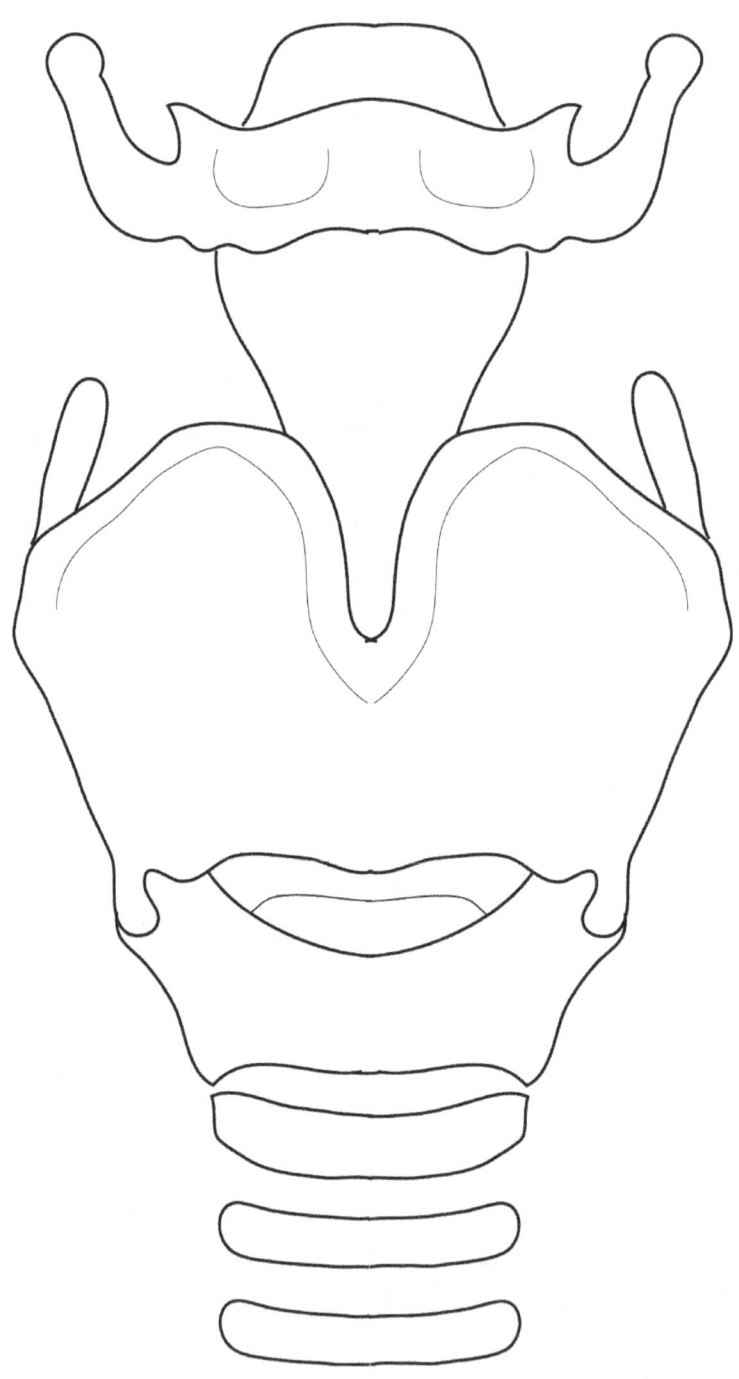

Colouring anatomy of the larynx 2

Colour and label the separate parts of the diagram

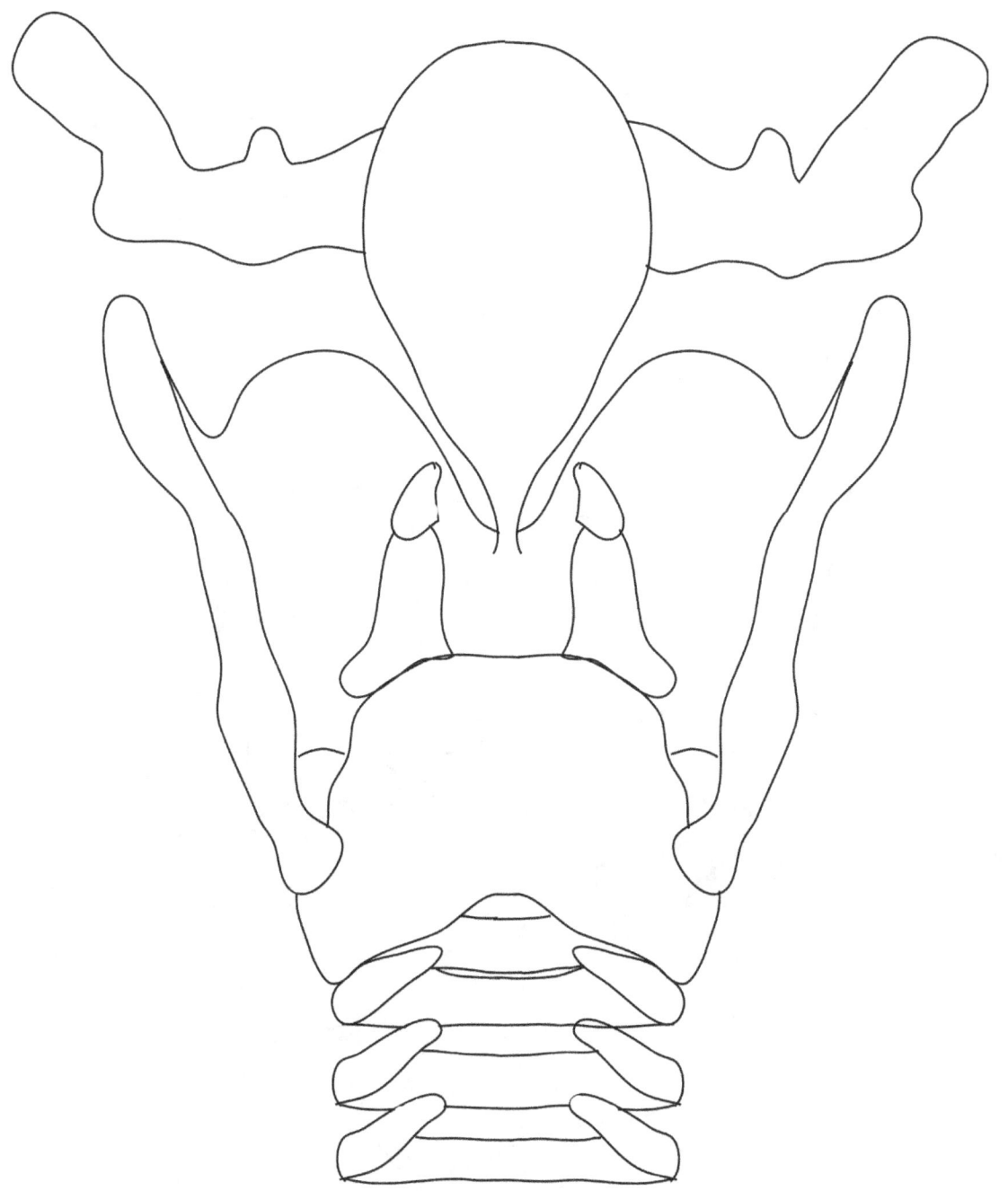

Colouring anatomy of the larynx 3

Colour and label the separate parts of the diagram

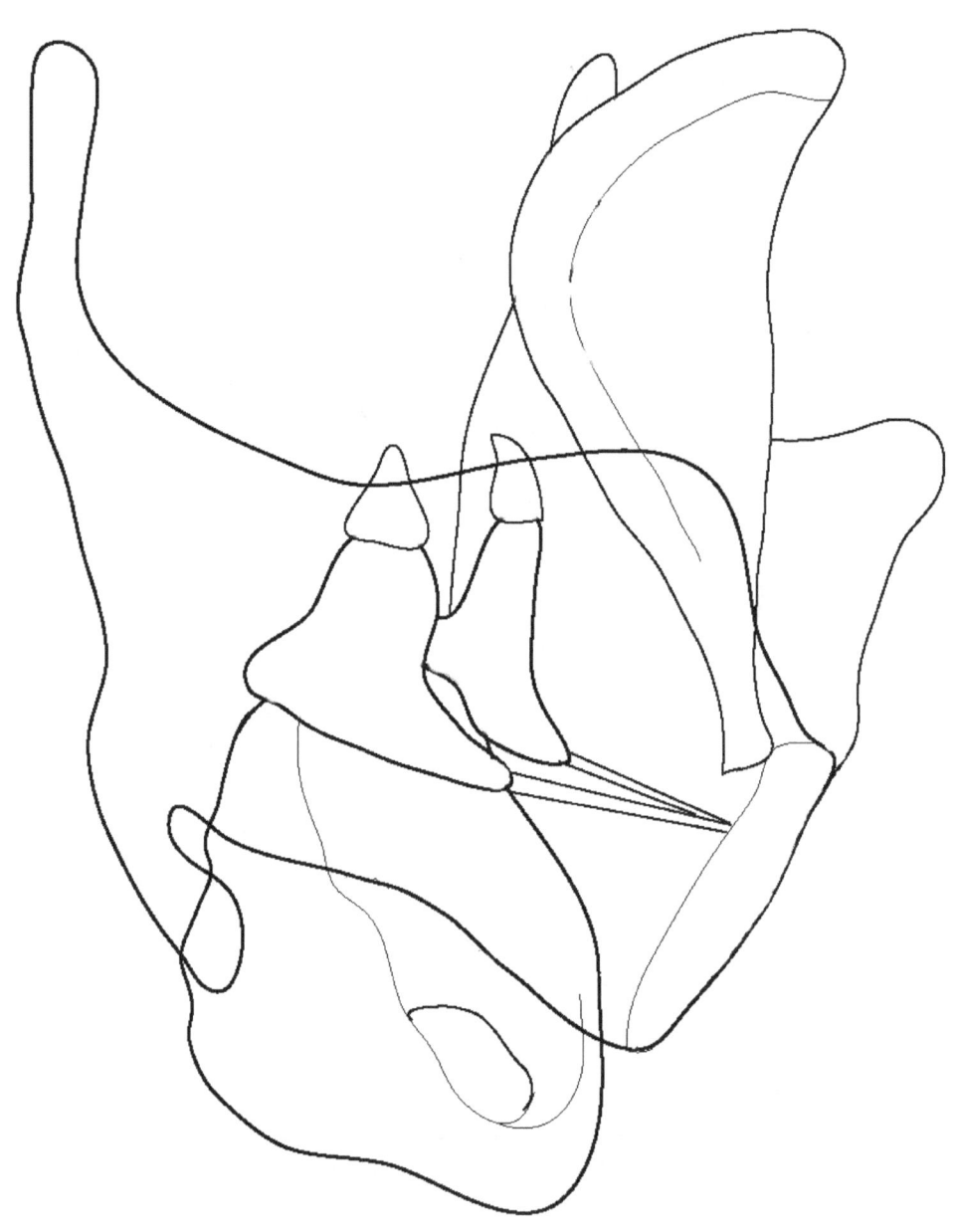

Colouring anatomy of the larynx 4

Colour and label the separate parts of the diagram

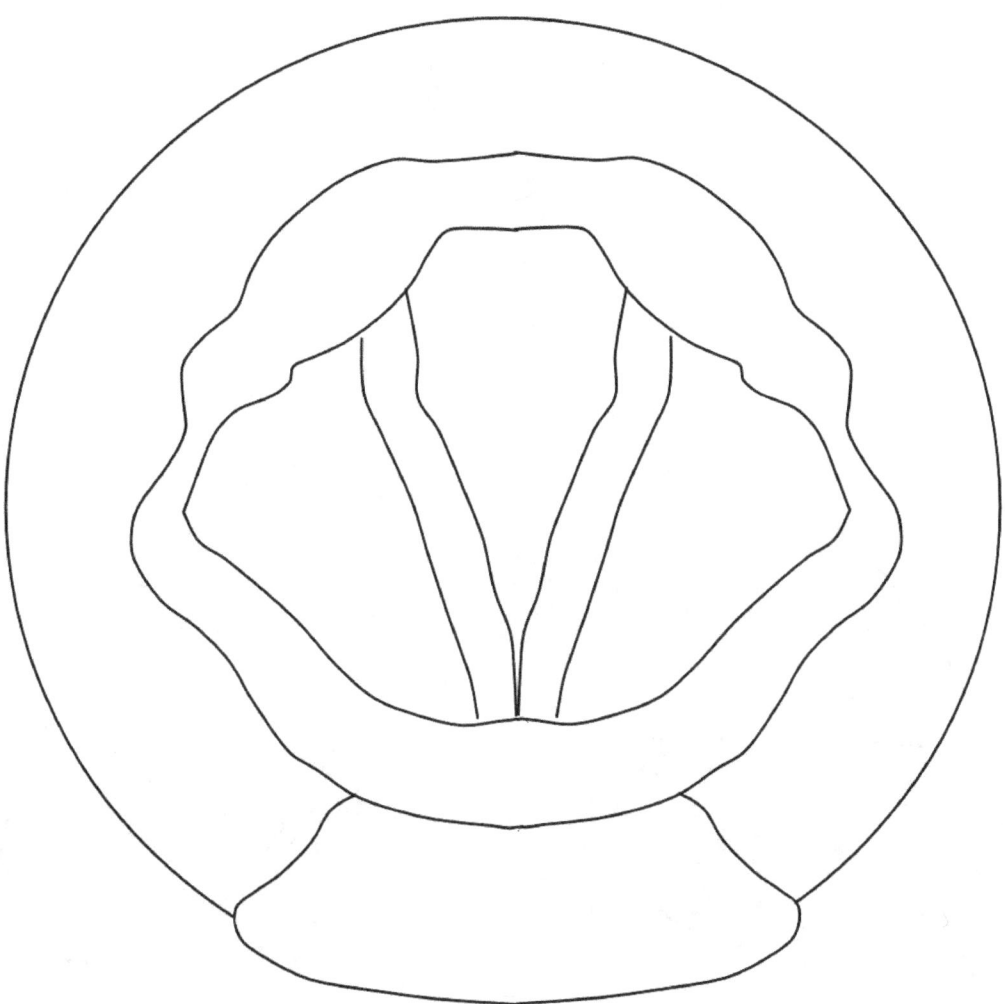

Colouring anatomy of the larynx 5

Colour and label the separate parts of the diagram

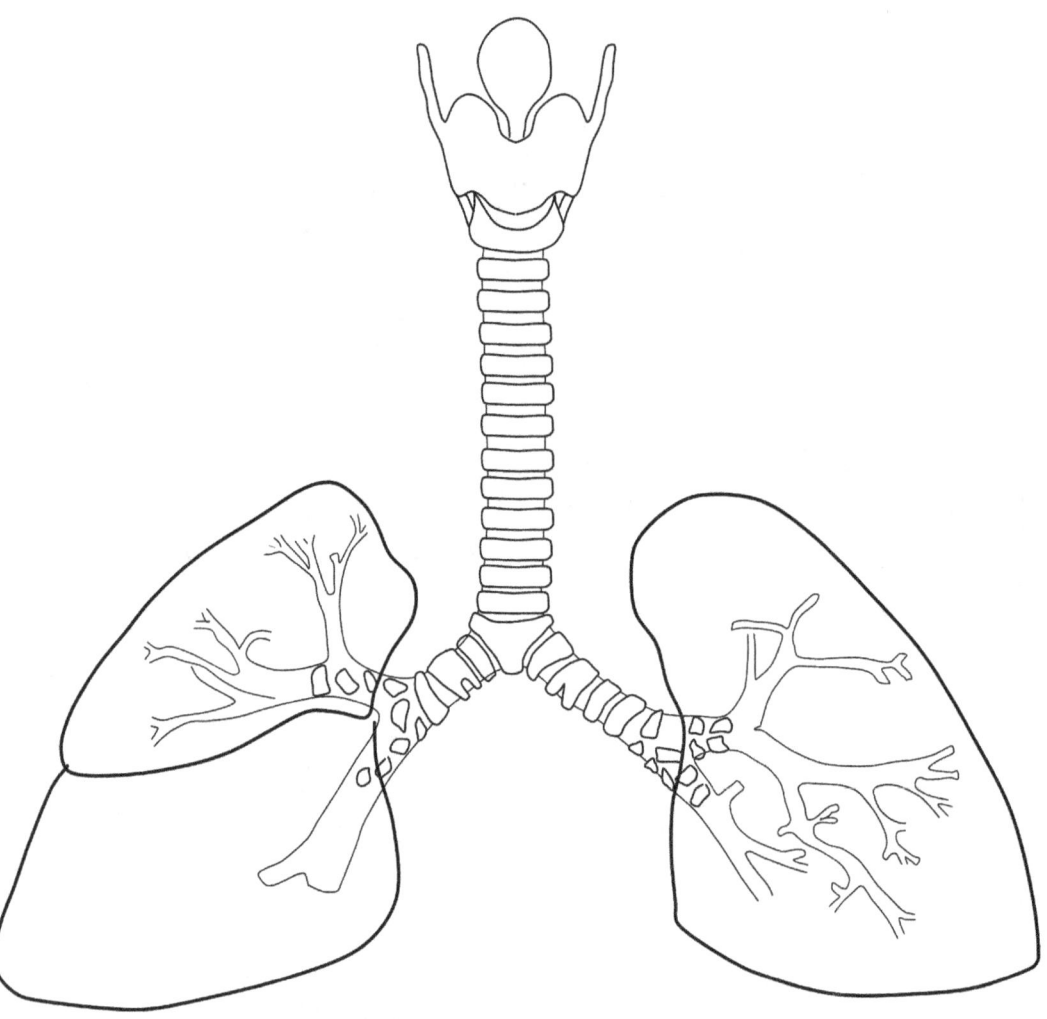

Section II: Muscles

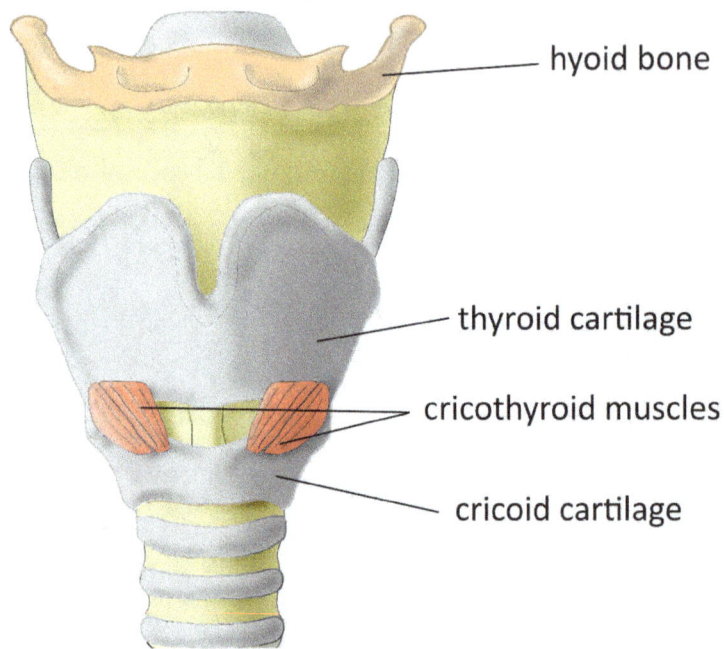

Front view of the intrinsic muscles

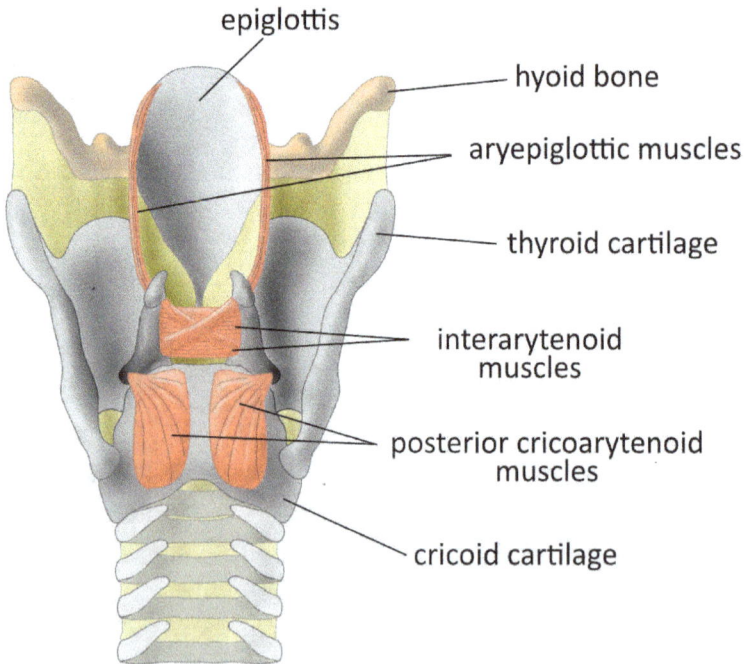

Rear view of the intrinsic muscles

Muscles of the larynx

There are two sets of muscles controlling the larynx. Those within the larynx are called the **intrinsic** muscles. Those outside the larynx are called the **extrinsic** muscles.

Intrinsic muscles

These are muscles that connect the laryngeal cartilages. Most lie inside the larynx except for the cricothyroid muscles which run externally between the **cricoid** and **thyroid** cartilages.
The **intrinsic muscles** are:

1. The **cricothyroid** muscles
2. The **posterior and lateral cricoarytenoid** muscles
3. The **transverse and oblique interarytenoid** muscles
4. The **aryepiglottic** muscles
5. The **vocalis** muscles and the **thyroarytenoid** muscles.

Some of these muscles (lateral cricoarytenoids, thyroarytenoids and vocalis) are not visible in the diagram because of their position within the larynx.

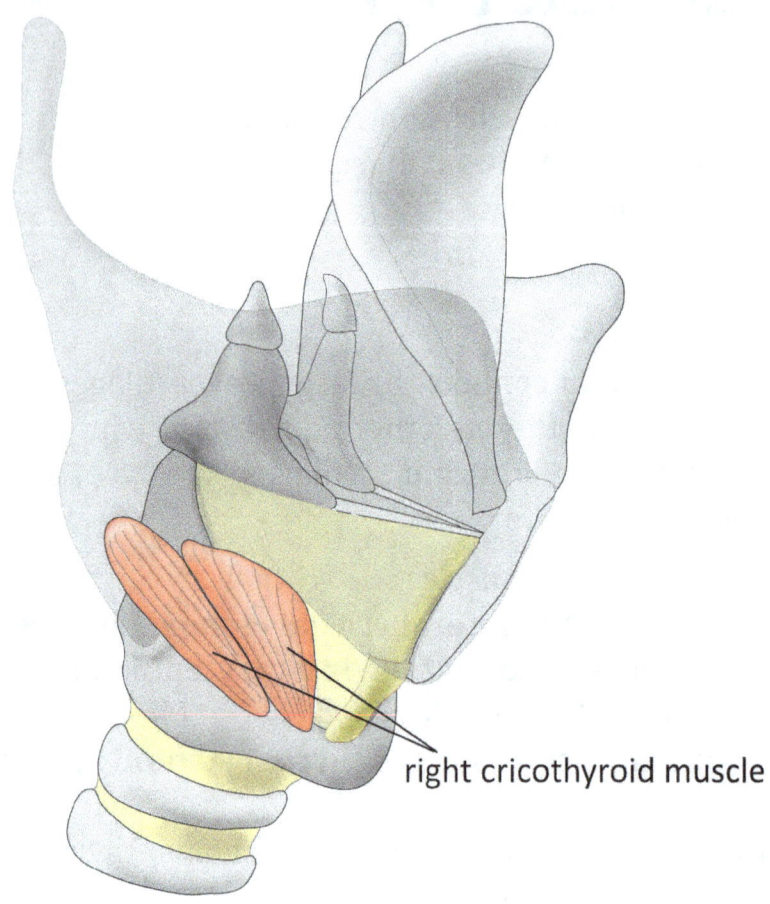

Side view of the cricothyroid muscle

Note: each cricothyroid muscle is divided into two parts. In this image, only the right cricothyroid muscle is shown.

Intrinsic muscles of the larynx

The cricothyroid muscles

Description
Unlike the muscles described so far, the **cricothyroid** muscles lie on the outer surface of the larynx. They run from the upper edge of the **cricoid** cartilage to the lower edge of the **thyroid** cartilage.

Function
The cricothyroid muscles **raise the pitch** of the voice by increasing the tension of the vocal folds. Although current scientific evidence suggests that this is achieved by tilting the cricoid cartilage **upwards** and **backwards**, there are many singers, particularly classical, who maintain that it is the thyroid cartilage that tilts downwards and forwards.

In either case, the action of the muscle will increase the distance between the attachment of the folds to the thyroid cartilage at one end, and to the arytenoid cartilages at the other end.

(See further discussion on cricoid vs thyroid tilting in Sections III and IV, and also: Unteregger *et al* (2017) 3D analysis of the movements of the laryngeal cartilages during singing. *Laryngoscope* **127**(7):1639–43.)

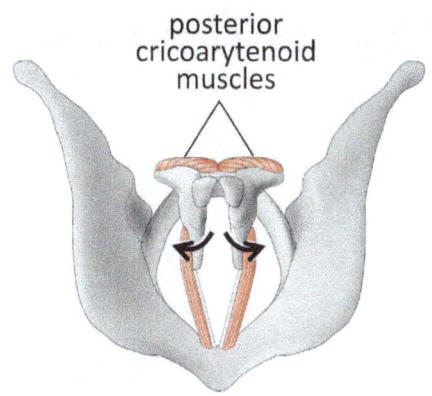

The lateral cricoarytenoid muscles seen from above

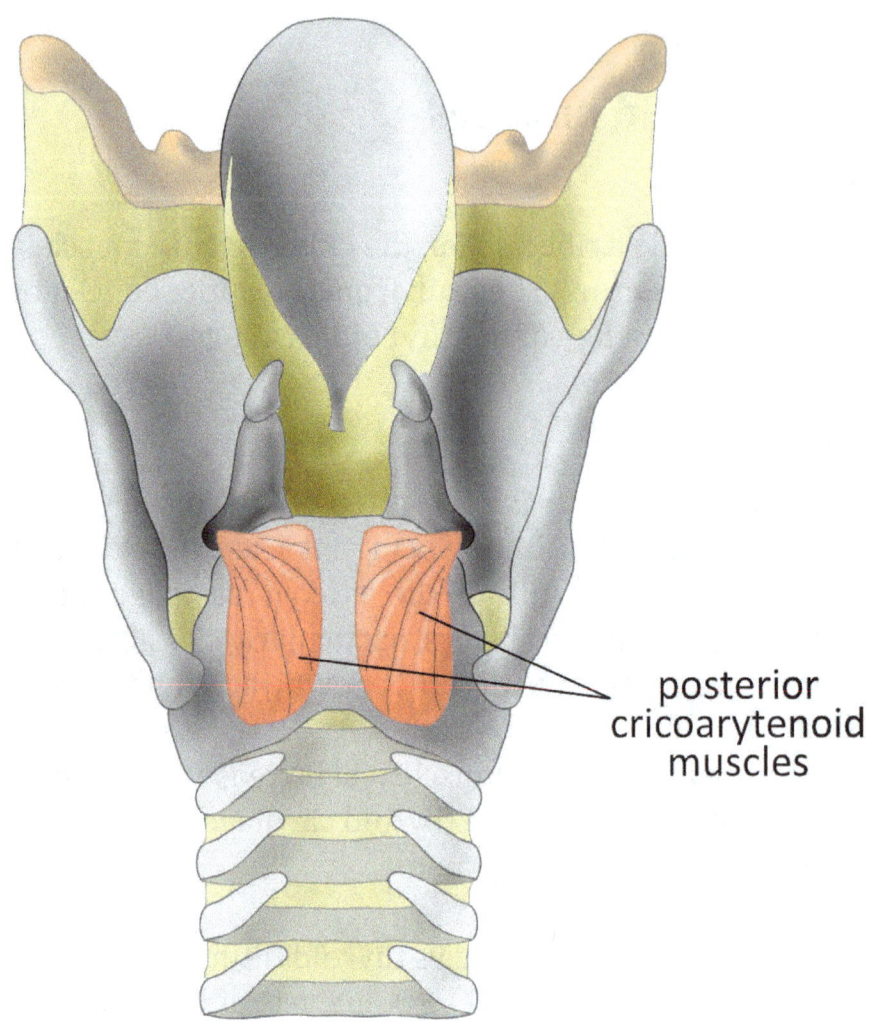

The posterior cricoarytenoid muscles seen from behind

The posterior cricoarytenoid muscles

Description

A large fleshy pair of muscles, rather like wings, on the rear surface of the **cricoid cartilage**. They are attached to the **muscular processes** of the arytenoid cartilages. This is one of the three processes on the arytenoid cartilages (see Section I).

Function

The posterior cricoarytenoid muscles **open** the vocal folds by rotating the arytenoid cartilages **outwards** to increase the space between the vocal folds (glottis). This enables air to be drawn through the larynx and into the lungs.

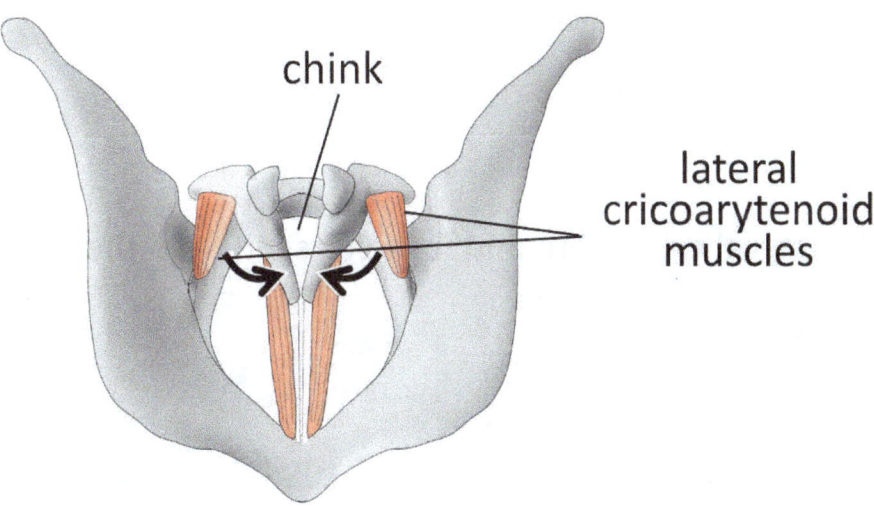

The lateral cricoarytenoid muscles seen from above

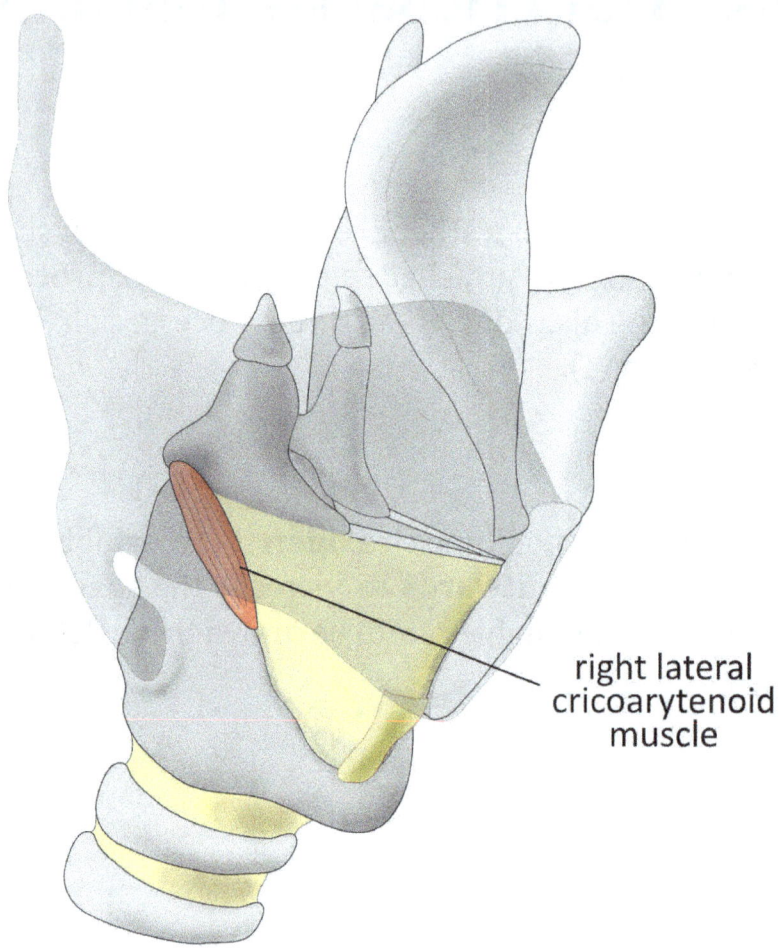

The lateral cricoarytenoid muscles seen from the rear

The lateral cricoarytenoid muscles

Description
These muscles are situated on the upper edge of each side of the cricoid cartilage. They attach the cricoid cartilage to the **muscular processes** of the arytenoid cartilages.

Function
The lateral cricoarytenoids have the opposite action to the posterior cricoarytenoids. They **close** the space between the vocal folds (glottis) by rotating the arytenoid cartilages **inwards**. This may leave a gap or 'chink' between the cartilages at the back of the vocal folds which will then require the further action of the interarytenoids to close fully.

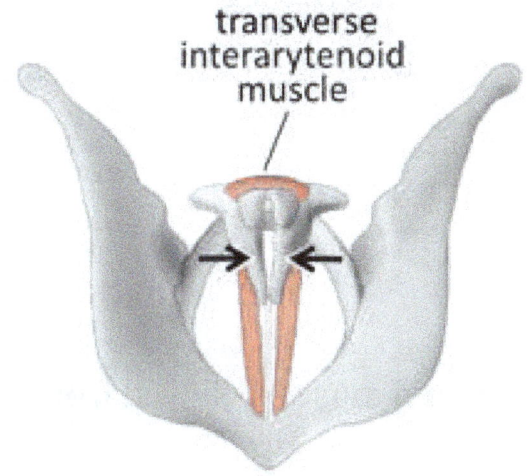

The arytenoid muscles viewed from above

Note: the transverse interarytenoid muscle is the only unpaired muscle within the larynx

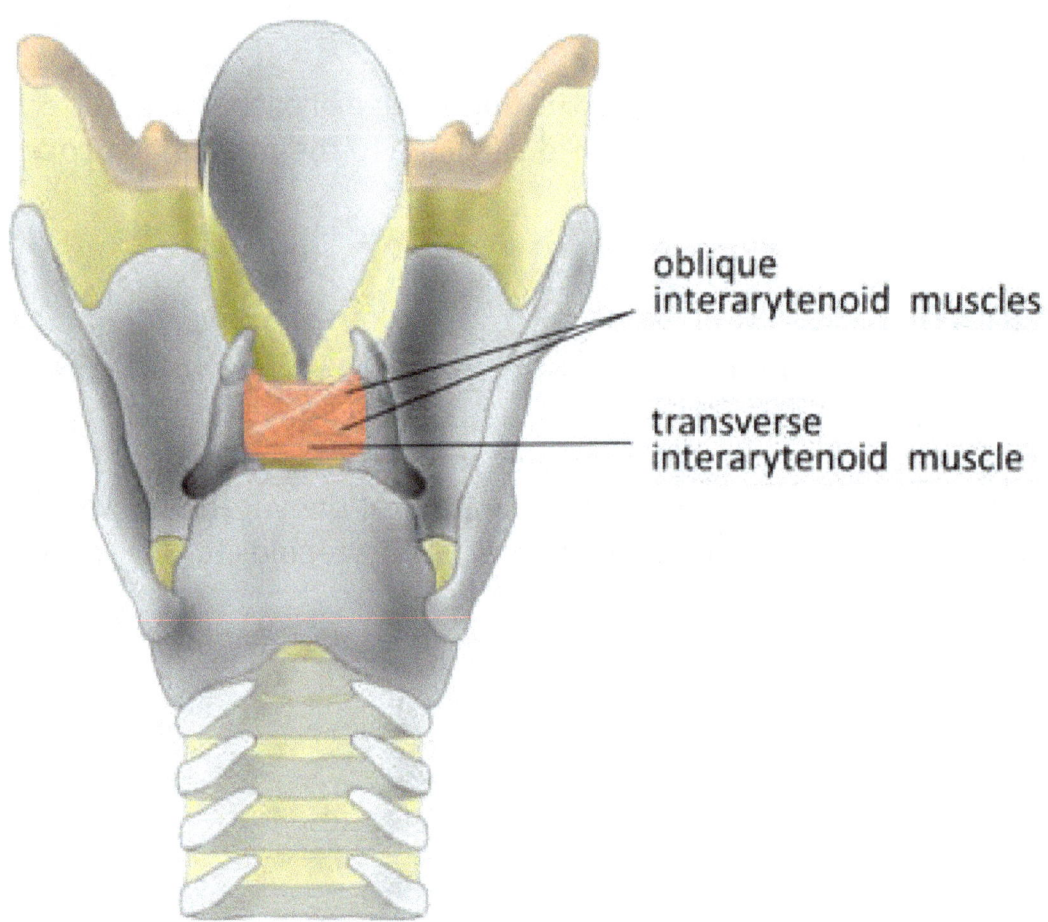

The arytenoid muscles viewed from the rear

The interarytenoid muscles

Description
The **interarytenoid muscles** run between the rear surfaces of the arytenoid cartilages from the **apical processes** downwards and are made up of muscle fibres that run in two different directions. One set runs **horizontally** and the others **cross obliquely**.

Function
The interarytenoid muscles **close** the gap at the back of the vocal folds to prevent air escaping during phonation.

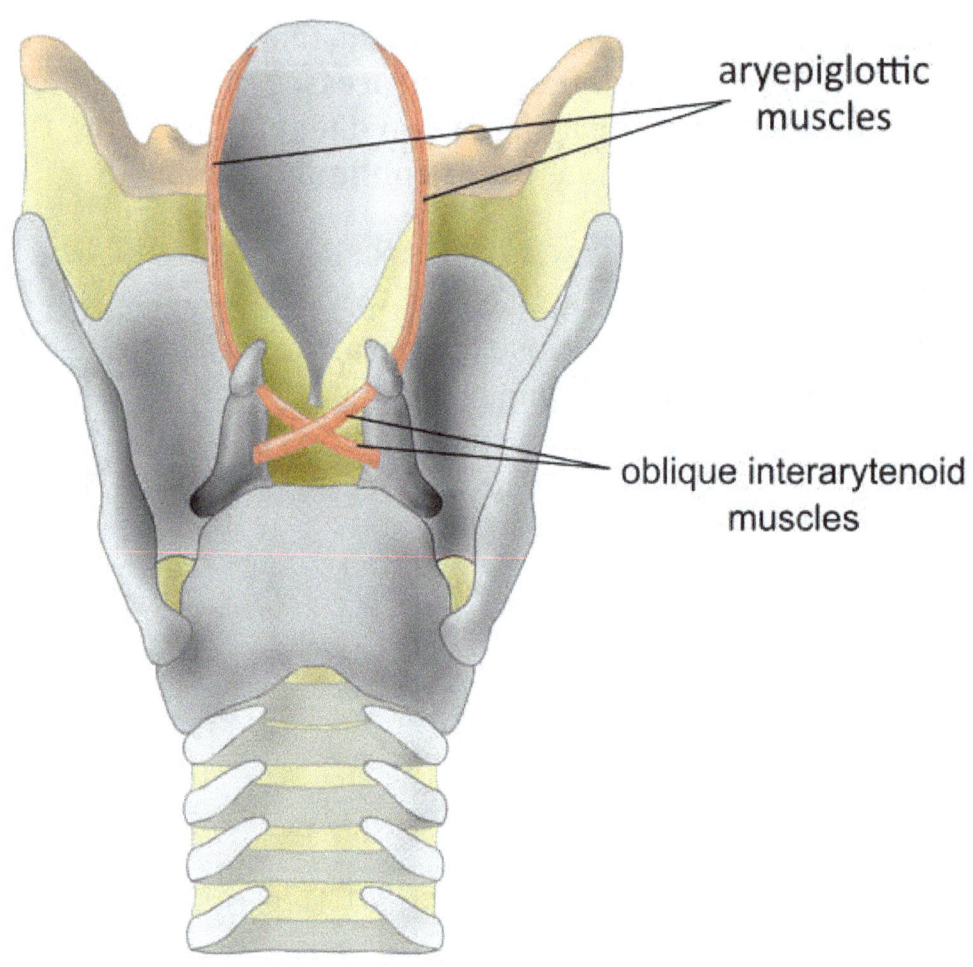

Rear view of the aryepiglottic muscles

The aryepiglottic muscles

Description
The **aryepiglottic muscles** run along the upper edge of the **aryepiglottic fold**. Together they form a purse-string around the opening of the resonant chamber of the larynx immediately above the vocal folds (vestibule). The aryepiglottic muscles are often said to be a continuation of the **oblique interarytenoid muscles**, and run upwards from the arytenoid cartilages to the epiglottis.

Function
The aryepiglottic muscles contain very few muscle fibres but they may play a part, in conjunction with other structures, in partially closing the upper end of the resonant chamber (vestibule) of the larynx. 33. For further information see section IV.

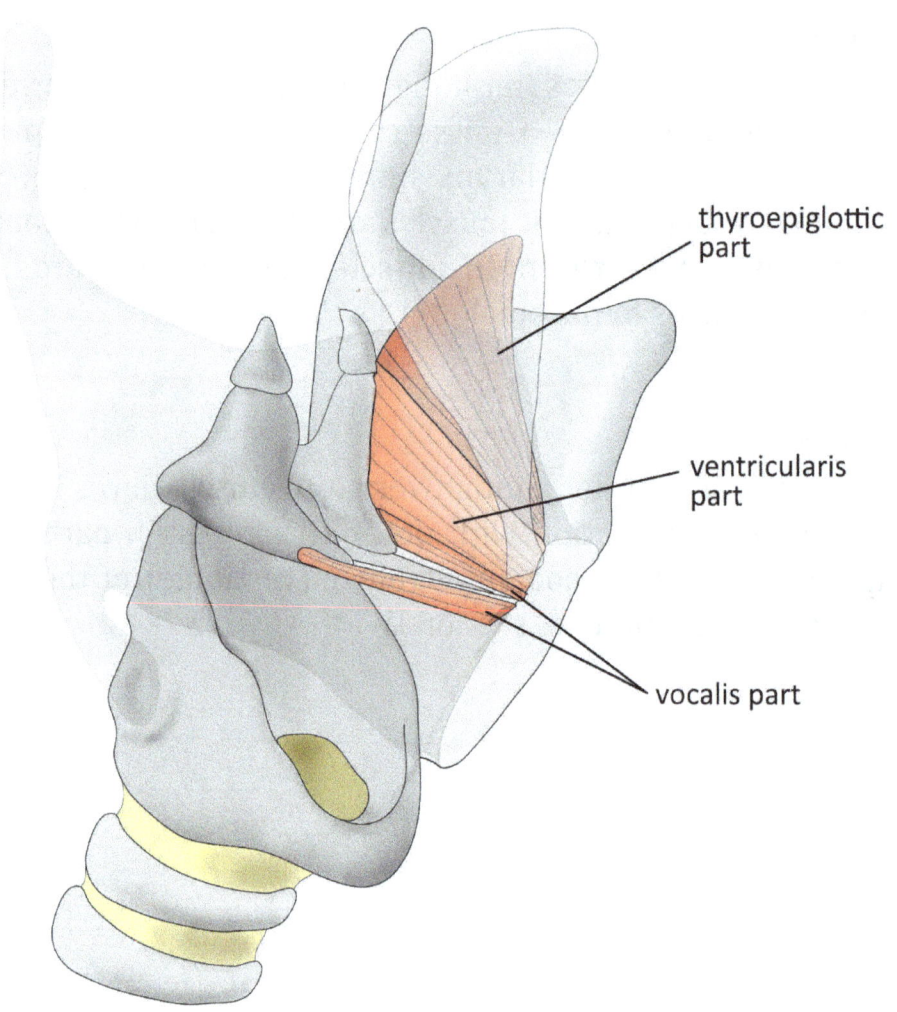

Side view of the thyroarytenoid and vocalis muscles. Three of the four parts of the thyroarytenoid muscle are visible in this view

The thyroarytenoid and vocalis muscles

Description

The **thyroarytenoid muscles** are vertical sheets of muscle that run from the inside of the thyroid cartilage to the **vocal and apical processes** of the arytenoid cartilages and to the epiglottis.

The thyroarytenoid muscles have several named parts. The use of these names can be inconsistent in both scientific and singing textbooks. The name is often used broadly to include all the parts of the thyroarytenoid muscles. Individually these are:

1. **Main body** of thyroarytenoid muscles.
2. **Vocalis muscles**: a horizontal ledge that emerges from each thyroarytenoid muscle and forms the core of the vocal folds.
3. **Ventricularis muscles**: the upper fibres of the thyroarytenoids that run lateral to the ventricular space and the false vocal folds.
4. **Thyroepiglottic muscles**: uppermost fibres of thyroarytenoid muscles. Although they are described as part of the thyroarytenoids, they do not run to the arytenoid cartilages but to the epiglottis.

For more information, the following papers are recommended. Moon J. and Alipour F. (2013) Muscular anatomy of the human ventricular folds. *Annals of Otology, Rhinology and Laryngology* **122**(9):561-7; Reidenbach M.M. (1998) The muscular tissue of the vestibular folds of the larynx *European Archives of Otorhinolaryngology* **255**(7):365-7.

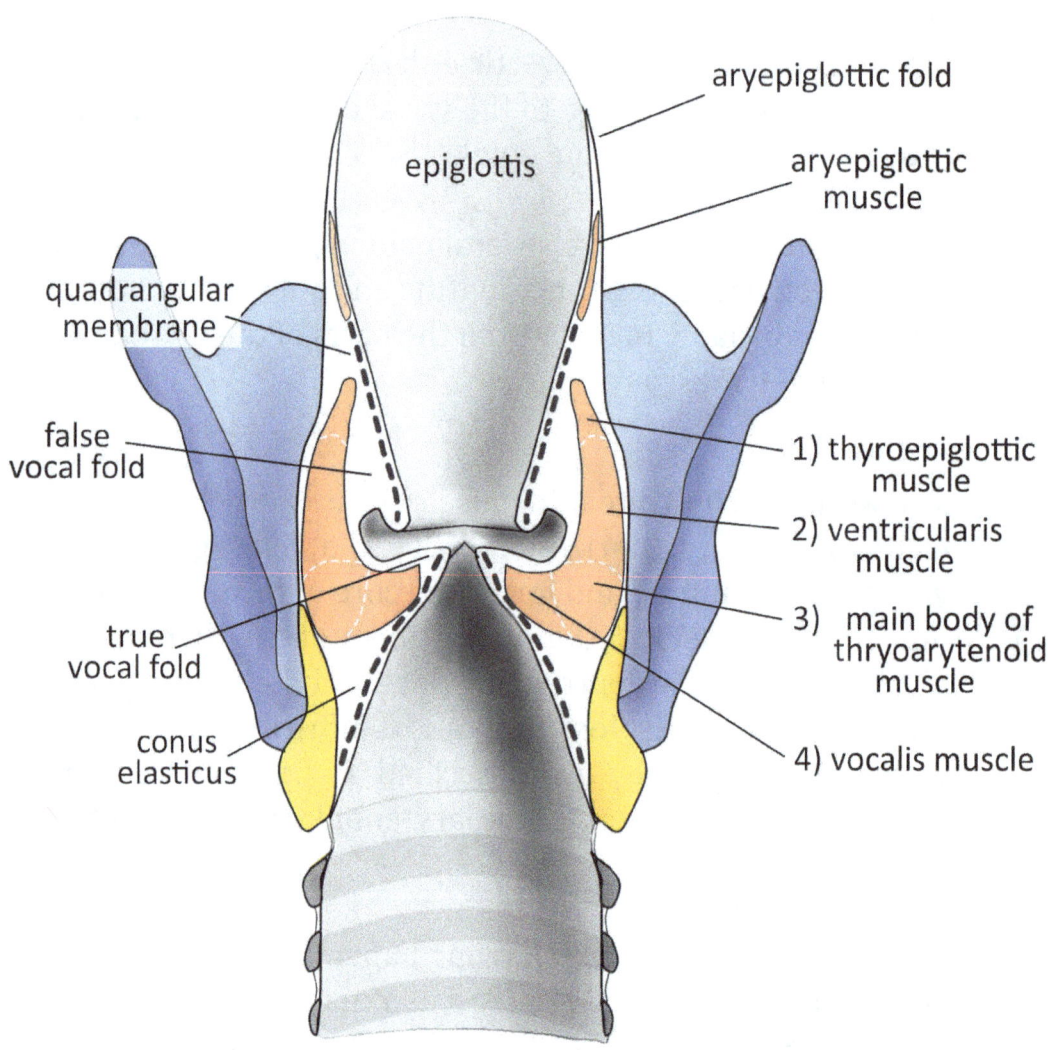

Coronal section of the thyroarytenoid muscles showing all four parts

The thyroarytenoid muscles

Function

1. **Main body:** The **thyroarytenoid muscles** reduce the pitch of the voice by **slackening** (reducing tension in) the vocal folds. When they contract, the distance between the arytenoid and thyroid cartilages is **shortened**.
2. The **vocalis muscles:** their action determines the timbre of the voice.
3. The **ventricularis muscles:** when these contract, they push the false vocal folds (also known as vestibular or ventricular folds) **downwards** and **inwards** towards the centre of the space (vestibule) above the true vocal folds.
   NOTE: The false vocal folds are made up of glandular and fatty tissue and contain very few muscle fibres.
4. The **thyroepiglottic muscles:** these pull on the upper edges of the aryepiglottic folds causing the upper opening of the vestibule to enlarge.

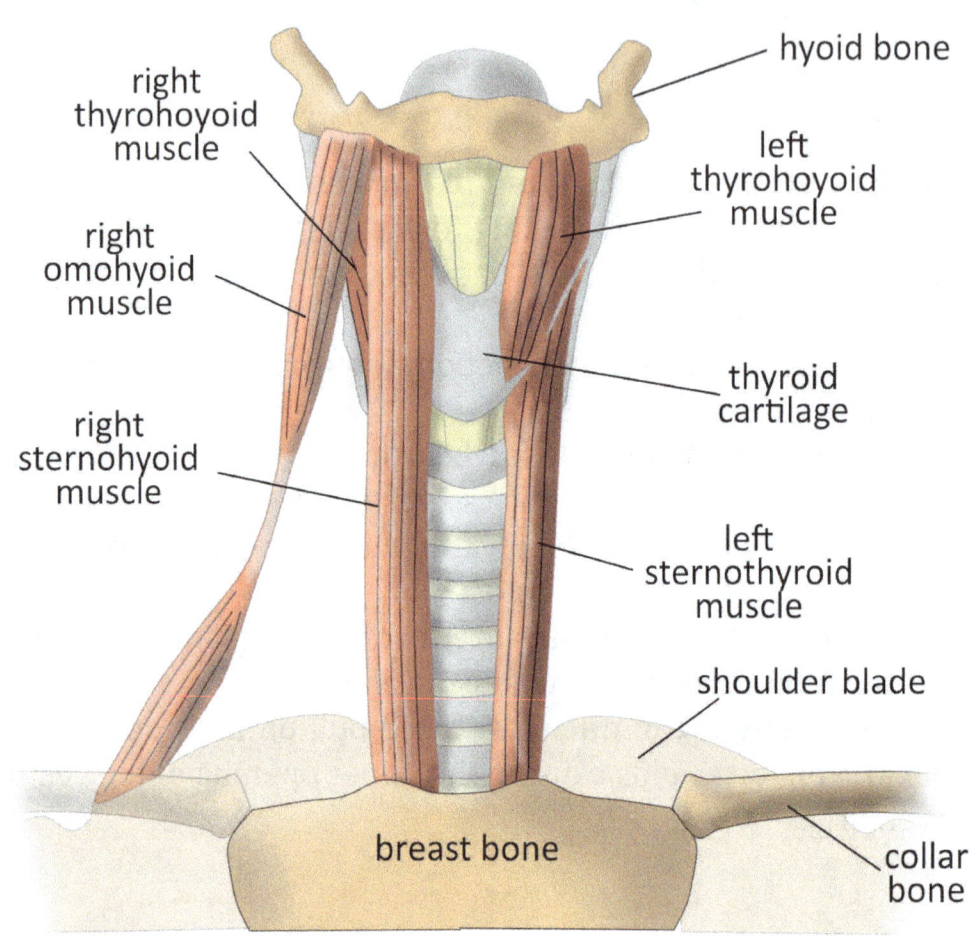

Front view of the extrinsic muscles of the larynx.

Note: the sternohyoid muscle on the left side of the diagram is not shown so that the muscles that lie behind it can be seen. The sternohyoid muscle is situated in front of both the thyrohyoid and the sternothyroid muscles.

Extrinsic muscles of the larynx

The extrinsic muscles all lie outside the body of the larynx. These muscles are involved in the movement of the larynx as a whole structure.

Although primarily involved in the act of swallowing, their function in vocalization is to **alter the length of the vocal tract**.
This change in length forms part of the complex mechanism that is involved in adjusting the resonant frequencies (formants) of the vocal tract.

1. When the larynx is **lowered**, these formant frequencies are reduced and the vocal timbre is **darkened**.
2. When the larynx is **raised**, the vocal tract is shortened and the timbre is **brightened**.

There are two types of extrinsic muscles: **direct** and **indirect**.
The **direct** muscles are attached to the larynx.
The **indirect** muscles are attached, not to the larynx, but to the hyoid bone, from which the larynx is suspended.

Direct extrinsic muscles
There are two pairs of direct extrinsic muscles:
>The **thyrohyoid muscles**
>The **sternothyroid muscles**

The thyrohyoid muscles
These run from the thyroid cartilage to the hyoid bone at the base of the tongue. They **raise the larynx** during swallowing and singing.

The sternothyroid muscles

These run from the sternum or breastbone to the thyroid cartilage and have the opposite effect of the thyrohyoid muscles.
They **pull the larynx downwards** during swallowing and singing.

Indirect extrinsic muscles

There are two pairs of indirect extrinsic muscles:
   The **sternohyoid muscles**
   The **omohyoid muscles**

The sternohyoid muscles

These run from the sternum or breastbone to the hyoid bone from which the larynx is suspended. They **pull the hyoid down**, and in so doing, lower the larynx.

The omohyoid muscles

These run from a notch on the upper edge of the scapula (shoulder blade) to the hyoid bone. They **pull the hyoid bone downwards and backwards** taking the larynx with them.

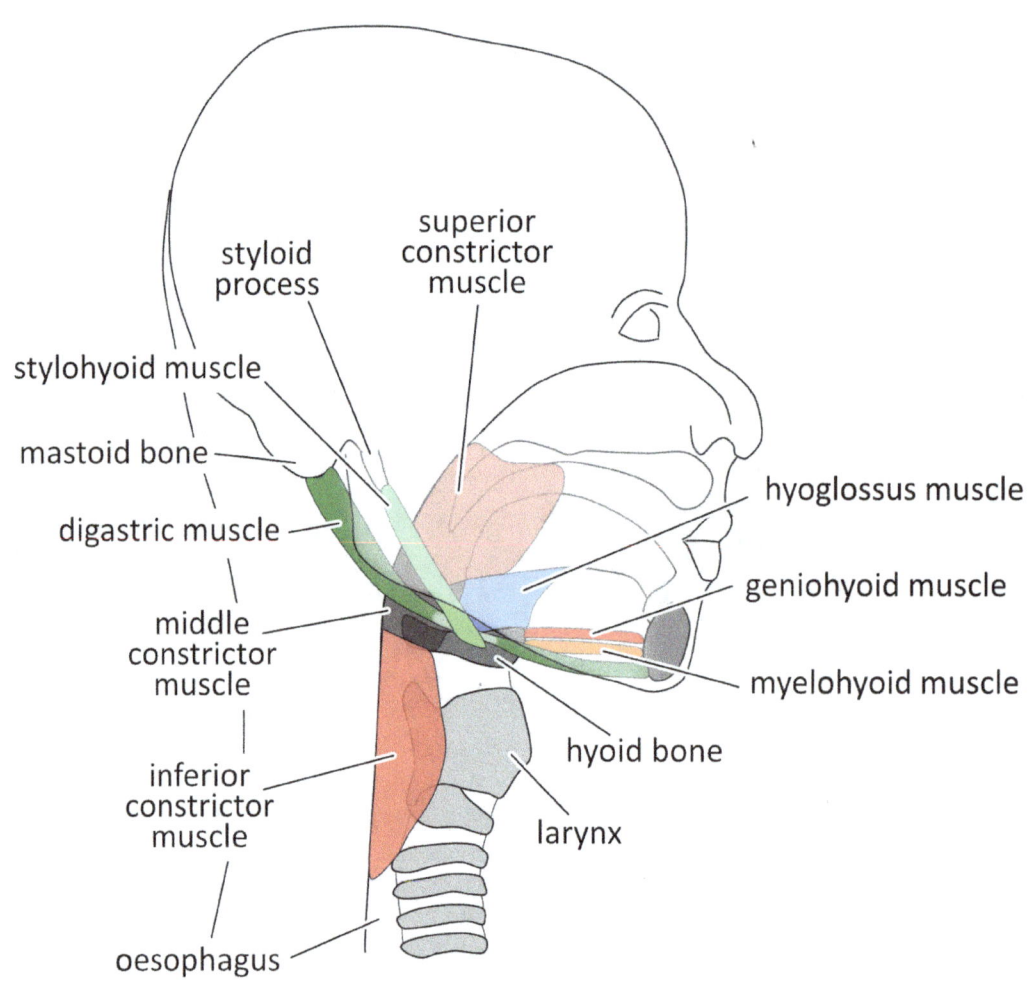

Side view of the other extrinsic muscles of the larynx

Other extrinsic muscles

These have an indirect relationship to the larynx and are either attached to the hyoid bone or surround the pharynx.

The primary role of these muscles is not to alter the position of the larynx, but to move the tongue and the jaw. Their attachment to the hyoid bone, however, may have a minor effect on laryngeal position. This would be a secondary consequence of their actions.

The stylohyoid muscles
These run from the styloid process at the base of the skull to the hyoid bone. They **pull the hyoid bone upwards**.

The digastric muscles
These are sling-like muscles that run from the mastoid bone behind the ear to the front of the jaw. Each muscle has two sections linked by a central tendon which is attached to the hyoid bone. **They maintain the jaw in an open position.**

The geniohyoid muscles
These run from the hyoid bone to the inner surface of the jaw. They **pull the hyoid bone forwards**. Because the root of the tongue is attached to the hyoid bone, this action pushes the tongue out.

The hyoglossus muscles
These run from the hyoid bone to the back of the tongue. Their function is to **depress the tongue and pull it backwards**.

The mylohyoid muscles

These lie between the geniohyoid muscles and the digastric muscles. They run from one side of the jaw to the other and form the muscular floor of the mouth. The back of the mylohyoid muscles are attached to the hyoid bone.

The pharyngeal constrictors

These are sheets of muscle that are wrapped around the pharynx and contribute to its wall. There are three pharyngeal constrictors: **superior, middle** and **inferior**.

The **superior** constrictor attaches to the muscular walls of the cheek (buccinator muscles) and has no relationship to the larynx.

The **middle** constrictor runs from one side of the hyoid bone to the other.

The **inferior** constrictor runs from one side of the larynx to the other. It is attached to both the **cricoid** and the **thyroid** cartilages.

These muscles may **narrow the pharynx** during singing, but their primary role is to **close the pharynx** completely when swallowing.

Questionnaire Section II

1. What is an 'intrinsic' muscle?

2. Name three of the intrinsic muscles of the larynx.

3. Which muscles open the glottis?

4. What do the lateral cricoarytenoid muscles do?

5. What is the function of the posterior cricoarytenoid muscles?

6. Name the two types of interarytenoid muscles.

7. How are the vocal folds slackened?

8. Name the pair of muscles that lie within the vocal folds.

9. How do we raise the pitch of the voice?

10. What is the function of the vocalis muscles?

11. What do the extrinsic muscles of the larynx do?

12. Which pair of muscles are used to raise the larynx?

13. What is the role of the omohyoid muscles?

14. Which pair of muscles connect the sternum and hyoid bone?

15. Name two structures attached to the vocal processes of the arytenoid cartilages.

Muscles of the Larynx wordsearch

```
K H X G E H O E Y Q P L B Q S K P E L H P O Z O
Z U E X T R I N S I C S J F A E O O A J M J U O
D Q F P B E T T K P Z B B R D V L N T I J R Z S
Z W F K Z A C P J E A E M V I M E D E F C H S G
M J N Q S T E R N O H Y O I D T E U R A D G P B
Z R R Z K W G P O O U L L M J R N C A R F D P P
J L K E D J Z A P G B E J Q R W T K L Y X Q T I
R P J D C I M K H P O S T E R I O R Z E T M I X
F Q I J J V B N P I N T R I N S I C F P H U X H
H F D B M M W A H I B E T K H A D H K I Y S J U
S G Y C R I C O A R Y T E N O I D R U G R A N T
G S B U B K N L Z K M X R Q D O F S C L O M I R
C T O C C W Q J V S R H Y S B C M M E O A J B E
G E X Y E E X N N C M Z X X Z H K R V T R J G S
B R D Q A Q U W D F M M M H Y O U D W T Y D N P
T N K K X L C P K C V N X O X B V X Y I T W U Z
U O S C A N K A Y Y Q J V Z M F R N T C E A Q A
T T X K T Q I N T E R A R Y T E N O I D N X N C
R H N K W M F O O M O H Y O I D V L N Z O A B O
O Y E J C M U P C K L S P W B T C I P O I E N B
F R S B R Q N P X A N T E R I O R E Y A D C E Q
I O S K V O C A L I S A A V R V M S L Z F E X S
P I E S N L D Y J F S A S D F N O N G F E Z C O
R D M K W Z A X J I J L W B Z G R R F Y K Q W H
```

Intrinsic	Interarytenoid	Sternohyoid
Lateral	Vocalis	Sternothyroid
Posterior	Omohyoid	Extrinsic
Aryepiglottic	Anterior	Thyroarytenoid
Cricoarytenoid		

Colour and label the muscles 1

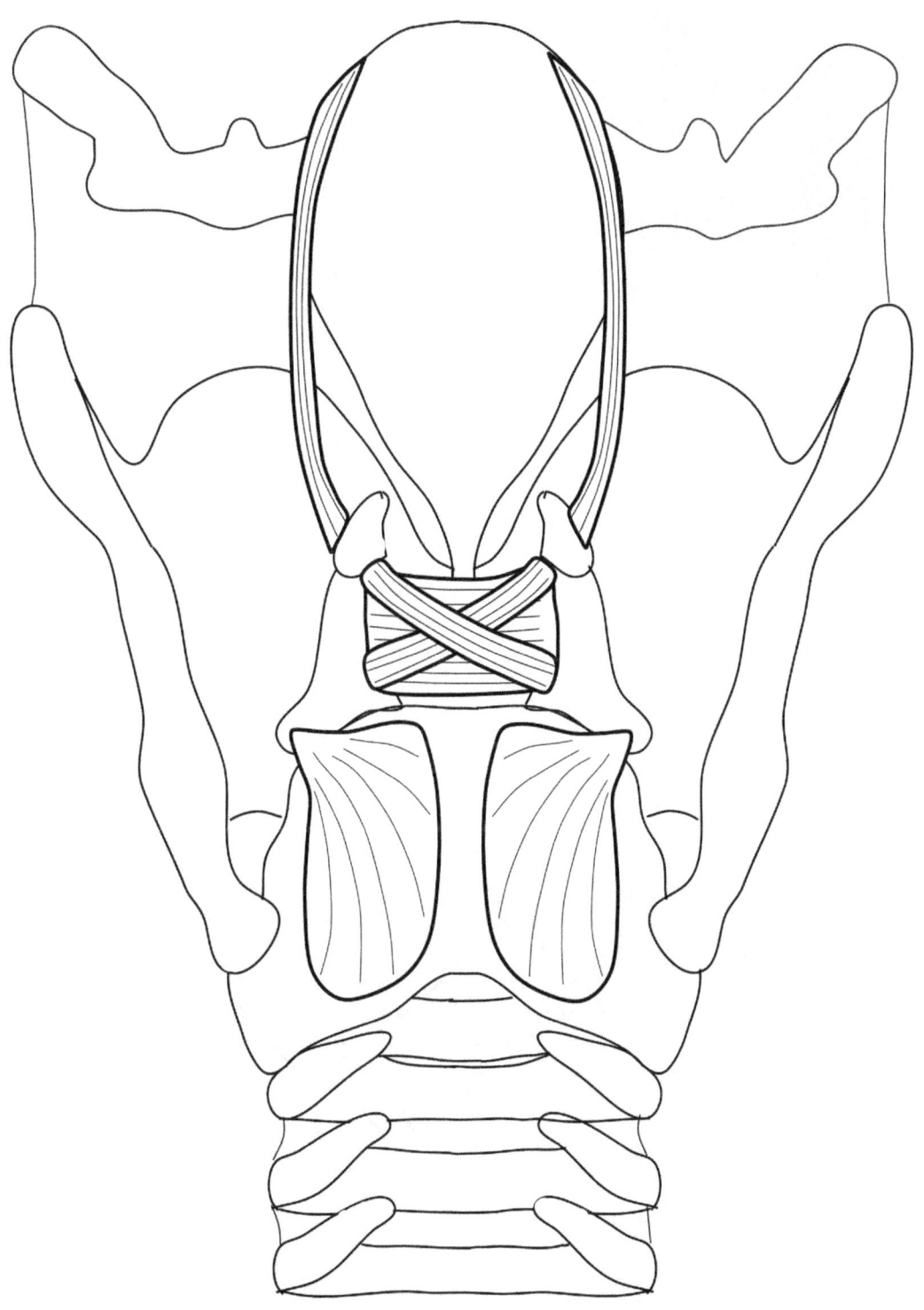

Colour and label the muscles 2

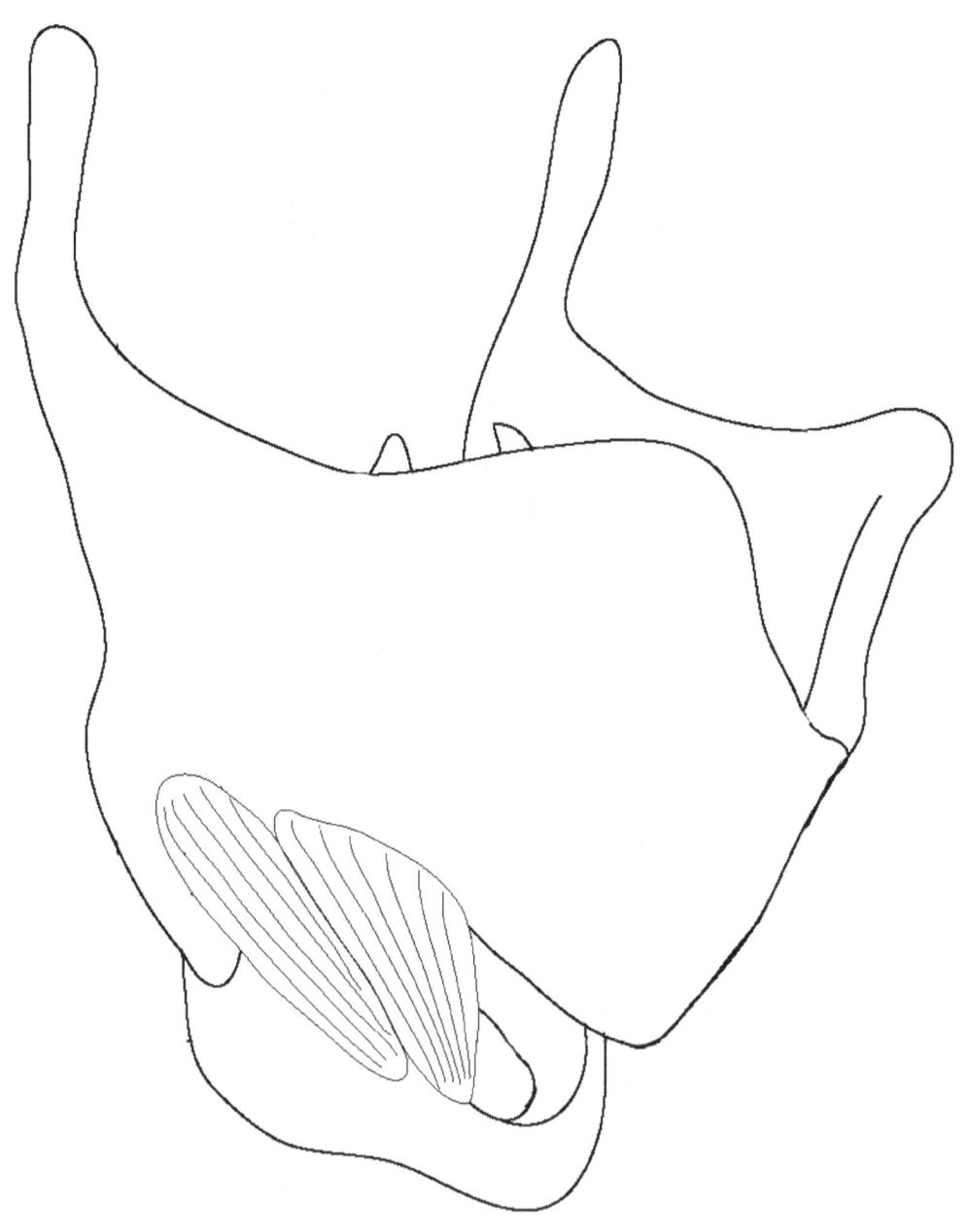

Colour and label the muscles 3

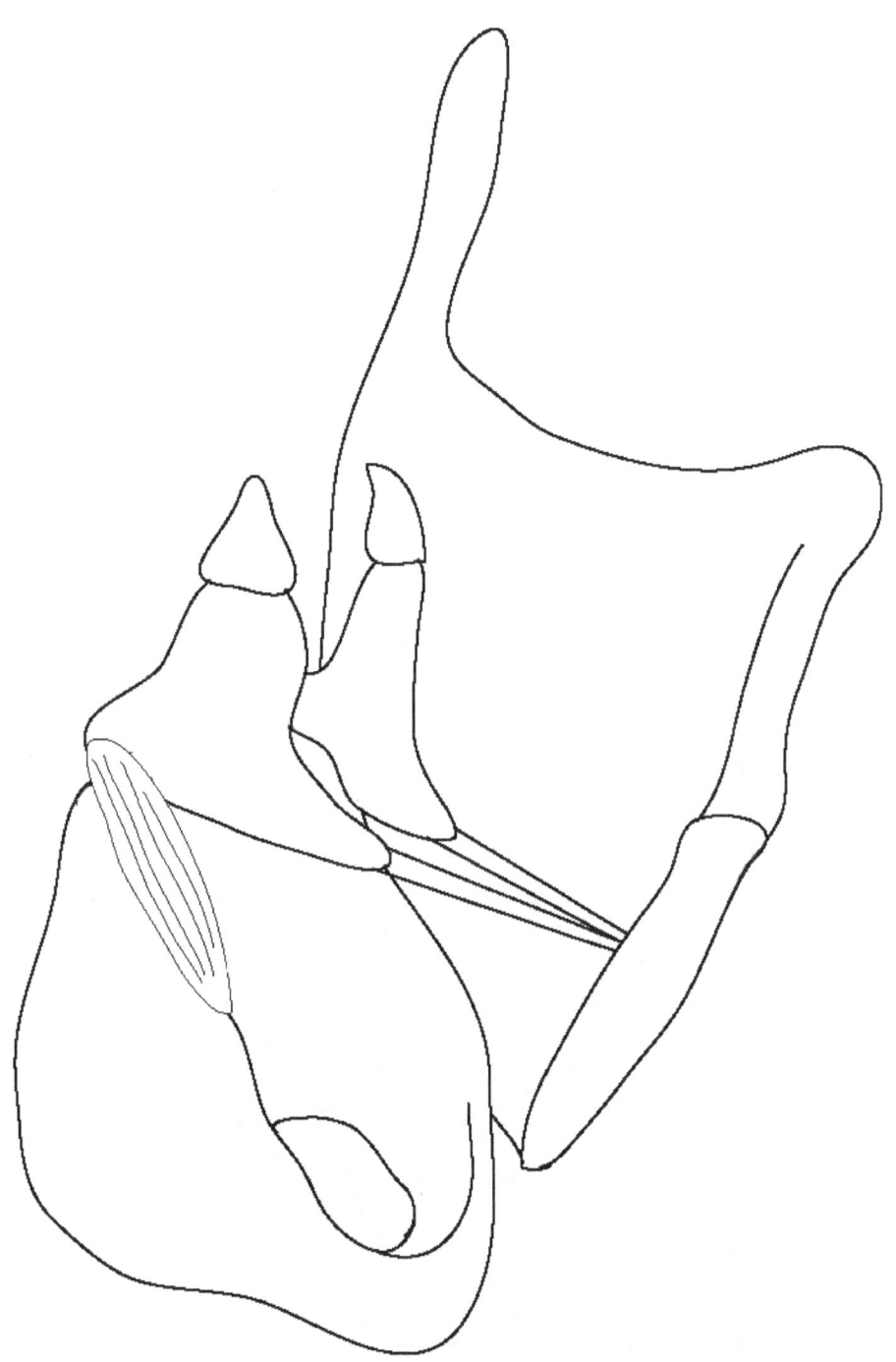

Colour and label the muscles 4

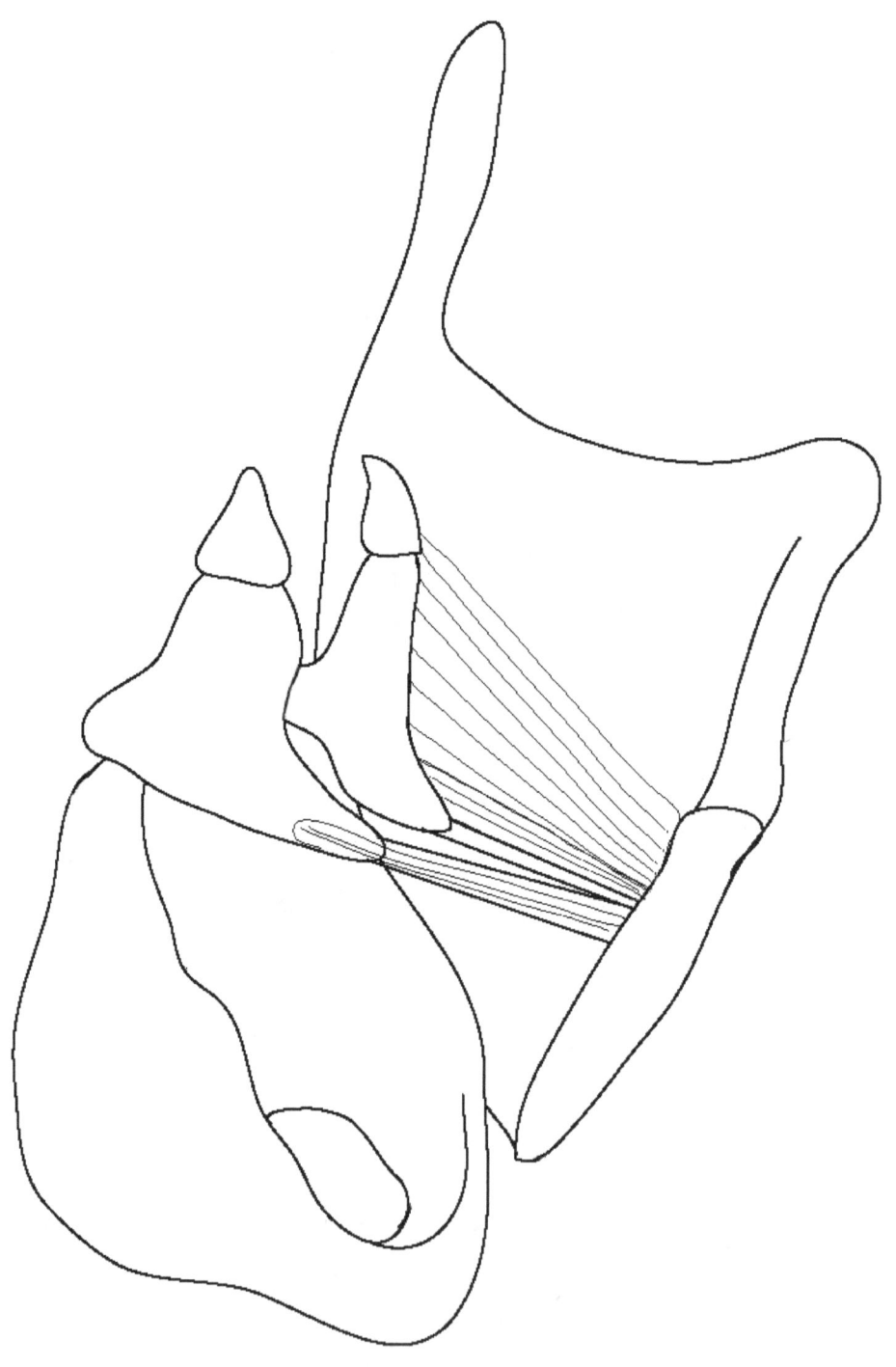

Section III The vocal folds

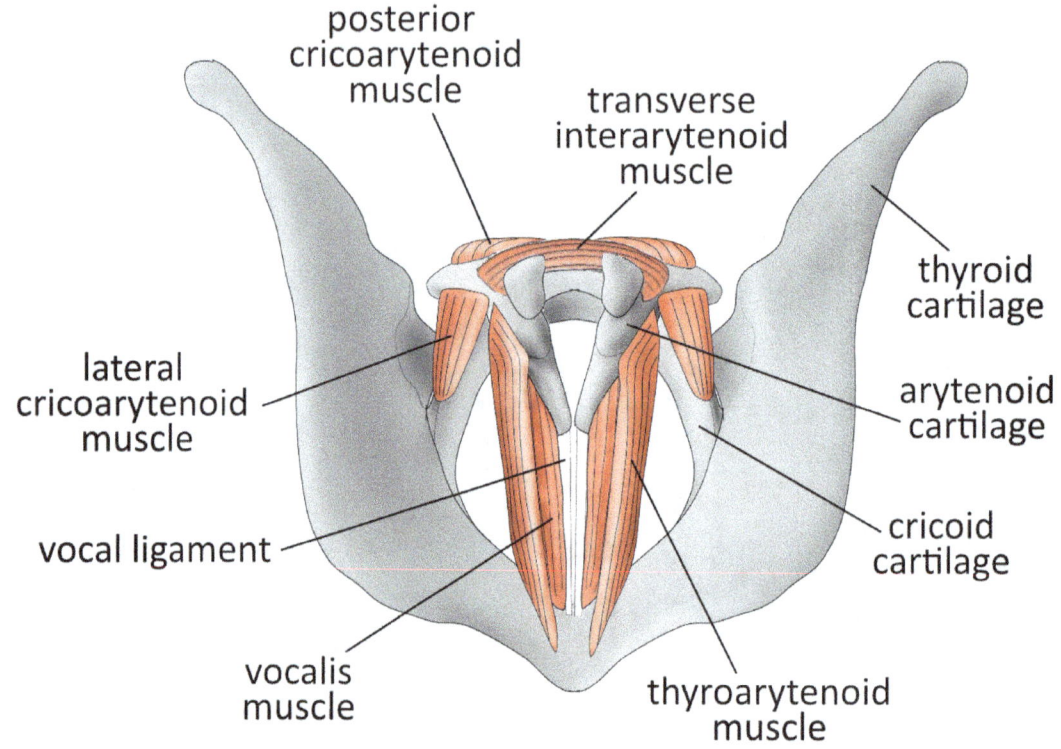

The vocal folds from above

The vocal folds

Description

The vocal folds are also traditionally known as the vocal cords. 'Folds' are a more accurate description of their appearance, however, and the term generally used by vocal anatomists. There are two **vocal folds** within the larynx. These are often called the **true vocal folds** to distinguish them from **the false vocal folds** which sit above them.

At one end, the true folds are attached to the inside of the thyroid cartilage and at the other, they are attached to the muscular processes of the arytenoid cartilages. The true vocal folds form two horizontal sheets of multi-layered tissue. Each contains a core of muscle known as the **vocalis** muscle. The vocalis extends outwards, rather like a ledge, from the long strip of muscle known as the **thyroarytenoid** muscle.

As with the whole internal surface of the vocal tract, much of the vocal folds are covered by a layer of tissue known as **mucosal epithelium**. This keeps the folds moist and supplies mucus to trap dust particles.

Note: there is another type of epithelium, known as squamous epithelium, on the edges of the vocal folds.

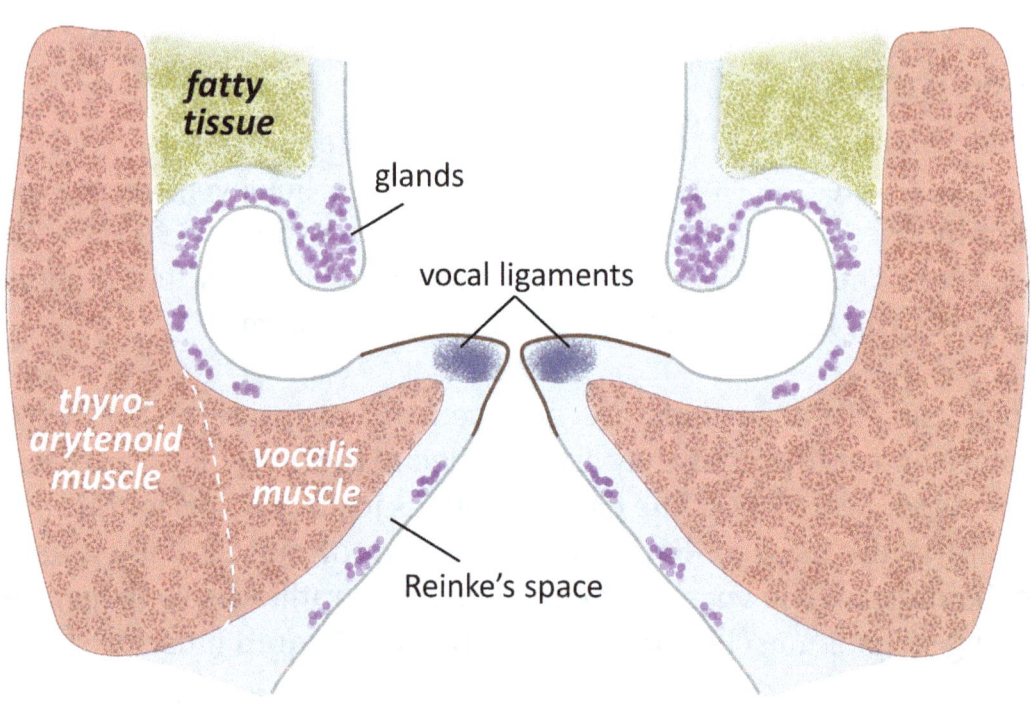

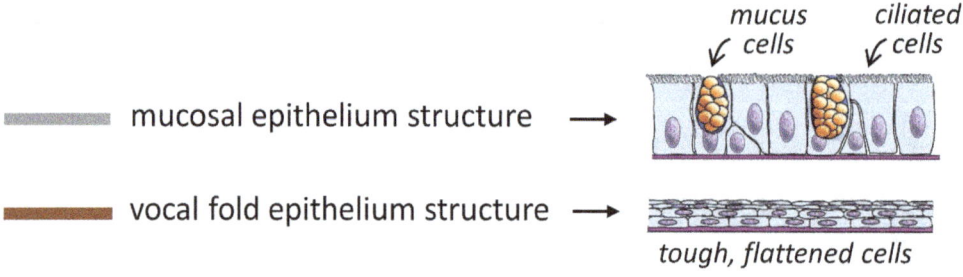

Coronal section of the vocal folds

Anatomy of the vocal folds

At the edges of both vocal folds the epithelium is toughened to protect them from damage as the folds constantly come together during phonation. This is known as the **free edge**. The epithelium covering the free edge does not secrete mucus.

Between the muscle and the epithelium is a layer of connective tissue composed of fibres of collagen and elastin, known as **Reinke's space**. This layer loosely attaches the epithelium to the muscular cores (vocalis muscles) of the folds and contains the **vocal ligaments.**

The vocal ligaments

Beneath the toughened epithelial layer at the edge of the vocal folds are the vocal ligaments. These are string-like structures that are made up of dense connective tissue. Together with the vocalis muscles, the vocal ligaments are stretched when either the cricoid cartilage tilts backwards or the thyroid cartilage rotates downwards.

Note: There is some disagreement about the movement of the cricoid vs the thyroid cartilage (see Sections II and IV). Many anatomical texts state that the cricothyroid muscle tilts the cricoid backwards, while others suggest that it primarily moves the thyroid cartilage. Some say that during phonation, the back of the cricoid is pressed against the vertebral column preventing cricoid movement so that instead, it is the thyroid cartilage that rotates downwards[1]. This is contradicted by a recent study using modern imaging methods that found only backward cricoid tilting from cricothyroid action with ascending pitch[2].

---

[1] Williams P.L. and Gray H. (1989) *Gray's Anatomy* 37ed. Edinburgh and New York, NY: Churchill Livingstone.
[2] Unteregger F., *et al.* (2017) 3D analysis of the movements of the laryngeal cartilages during singing. *Laryngoscope* **127**(7):1639–43.

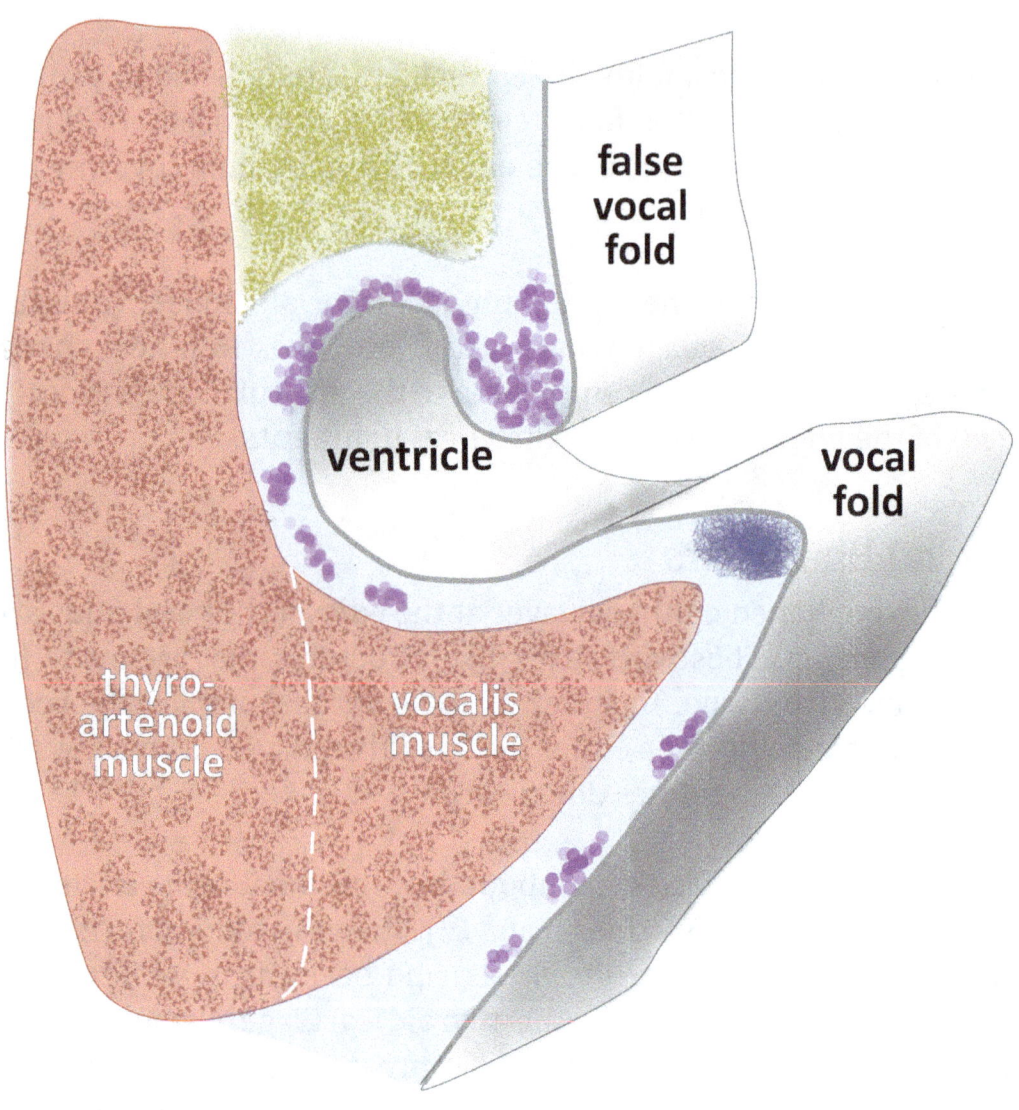

3D coronal section of the ventricle and false vocal folds

The false vocal folds and the ventricles

Above the true vocal folds lie the **false vocal folds** (also known as vestibular or ventricular folds). They are covered by mucosal epithelium. The bulk of the false folds is composed of fatty tissue and glands held together by fibres of collagen and elastin. They contain very few muscle fibres and are rarely involved in singing (see section IV).

Between the true vocal folds and the false vocal folds are narrow cavities in the wall of the larynx known as the **ventricles**. These are lined with mucus-secreting glands.

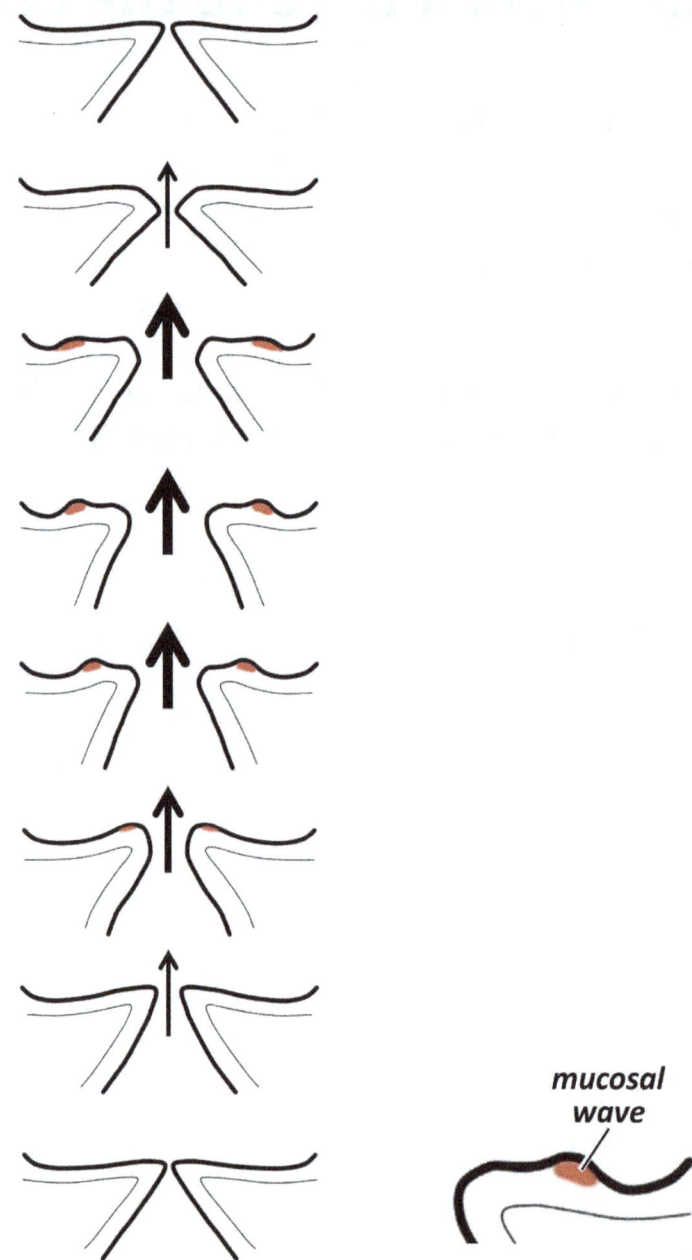

Cycles of vocal fold motion during phonation, showing the mucosal wave

Movement of vocal folds

When taking a breath, the vocal folds move apart to open the glottis. For vocal sounds to occur, the vocal folds come together and the glottis is closed. Sound is created by the rapid opening and closing of the vocal folds. This is driven by the breath.

The stages of vocal fold movement during phonation
1. The pressure rises beneath the closed vocal folds.
2. This pushes the folds apart.
3. As the folds open further, the air moves faster and the pressure between the vocal folds falls, drawing them together.
   This is known as the **Bernoulli Effect**.
4. Closure is aided by the elasticity of the vocal folds. As can be seen in the figure, the deeper parts of the vocal folds come together first. This makes the edges appear rounded at this stage of the cycle.
5. This cycle is then repeated.

Note: further information on vocal fold movement during singing can be found in Section IV.

The mucosal wave
As the air pushes the vocal folds apart, the epithelium or mucosa on the upper surface is thrown outwards from the edge of the folds like a wave. This is because the epithelium is only loosely attached to the underlying vocalis muscles by fibres in Reinke's space. The mucosal wave assists the opening of the folds.

Note: To ensure free movement of the mucosal wave, the folds should be kept well hydrated by drinking plenty of water.

Questionnaire section III

1. Where are the vocal folds situated?

2. Which structures are they attached to?

3. What covers the surface of the true and false vocal folds?

4. What forms the central core of the vocal folds?

5. How are the edges of the vocal folds protected?

6. What is the name of the space that lies beneath the epithelium. covering the vocal folds?

7. What is the vocal ligament?

8. Where do the vocal ligaments lie?

9. What is the driving force for vocalisation?

10. What causes the Bernoulli Effect?

11. Why is 'the mucosal wave important?'

12. What lies between the true and the false vocal folds?

13. What is the role of the mucosal epithelium?

14. List the stages of vocal fold movement.

Colouring anatomy of the vocal folds 1

Colour and label the separate parts of the diagram

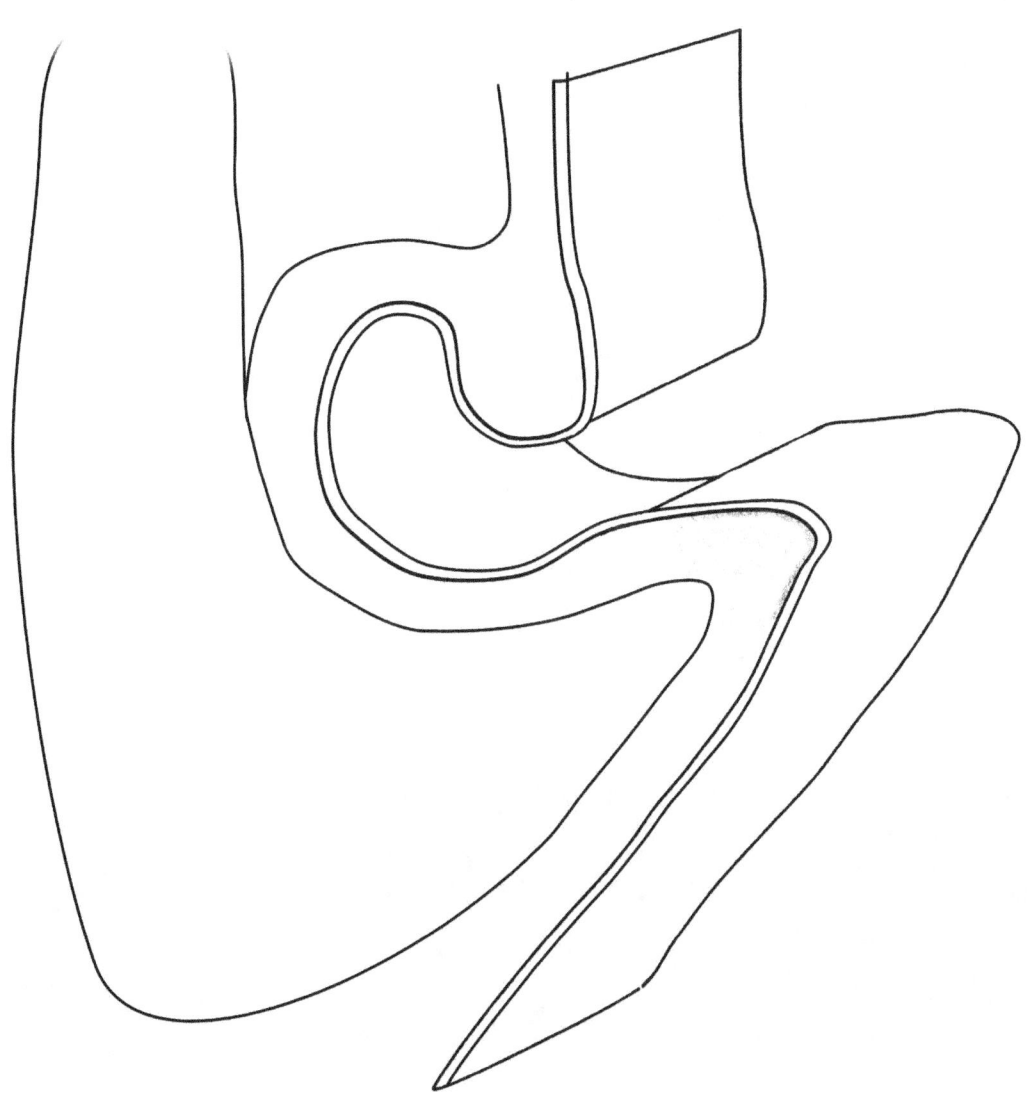

Colouring anatomy of the vocal folds 2

Colour and label the separate parts of the diagram

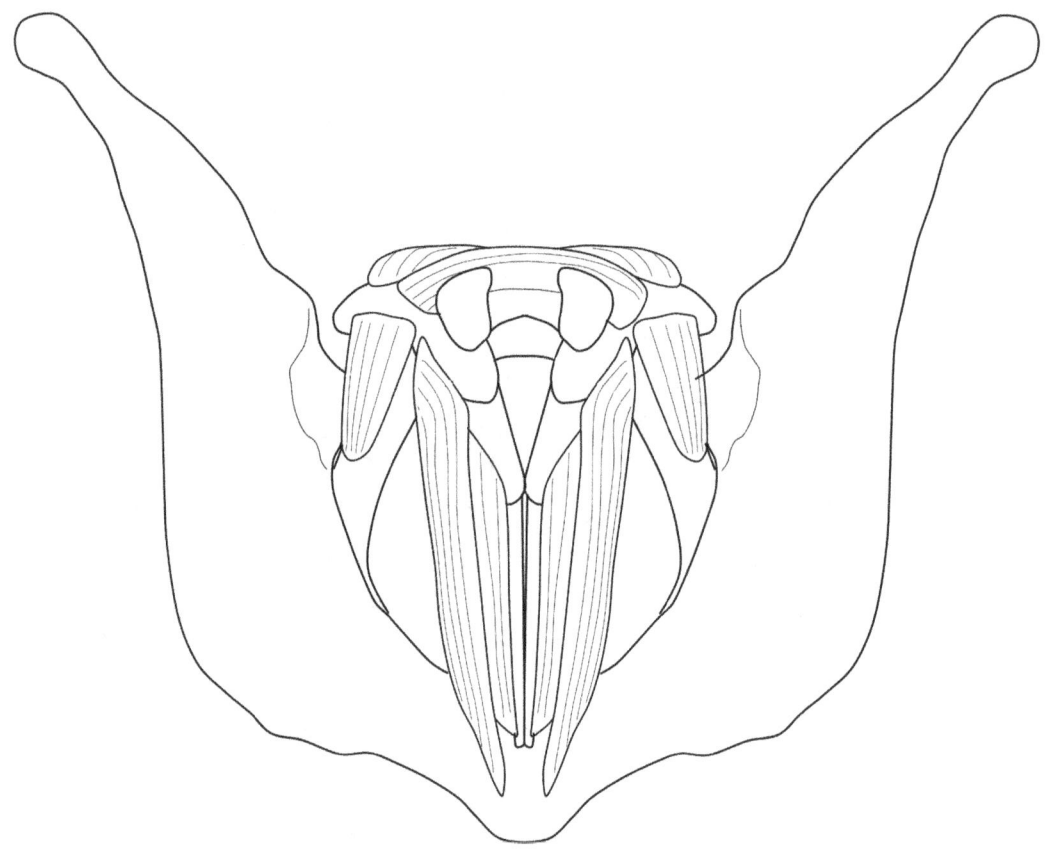

Word matching

Draw lines to pair the correct anatomical terms related to the vocal folds.

Vocal	Muscle
Bernoulli	Space
Mucosal	Edge
Reinke's	Tissue
Vocalis	Folds
Thyro-	Effect
True	Arytenoid
Vocal	Ciliated
Free	Folds
Connective	Wave
Cells	Ligament

Word scramble

Unscramble the following terms

1. OAVCL DFSLO _____

2. CSLMAUO VEWA _____

3. UEMTEPILHI _____

4. ACOVL TNLGIEAM _____

5. EOLNBURIL EECFTF _____

6. OITLGTS _____

7. ORHTIDY TAACGILER _____

8. HINTAONPO _____

9. TONADYIER GEATCAILR _____

10. SLANTIE _____

11. LUEBISTVE _____

12. EVRTECSNIL _____

13. ACOILSV _____

14. ALNRYX _____

Answers

1. Vocal folds. 2. Mucosal wave. 3. Epithelium. 4. Vocal ligament. 5. Bernoulli effect. 6. Glottis. 7. Thyroid cartilage. 8. Phonation. 9. Arytenoid cartilage. 10. Elastin. 11. Vestibule. 12. Ventricles. 13. Vocalis. 14. Larynx.

Vocal folds word search

```
M I B E R N O U L L I D R I F H L G Z J Z F A I
R W G H M H M S I R H Z C Z U A R Y T E N O I D
E H O V Y C F C D Z L O P R T E P Y Y T W L E W
I B G G E H V R J V P M U H I C R Z K W V C D A
N C E I M N W H O Q C O R G L L L K U N Q I X Z
K F W Y V O C A L F O L D O T P H O N A T I O N
E A L I G A M E N T K Q C E L L S R M N F G J N
S Z Z M B L V H P G P B T J X K B E F N D L X P
G L Y W F P E E T N V C D P H N L J A N N O E C
V P I T C H N P O D L H V A M V O C A L G T D U
F I A O S Q T I E P M O Y F H J F J Q P F T T E
N S I Q C Y R T W H M B L W K C V O C A L I S K
I D X Z D K I H Y P J T C I L I A T E D W S N N
L I Q A M G C E Y Q D L O N W J L W Z W Z P F M
U W C V U N L L Q G A H P U S O C F K A A W K S
O H F I B A E I R G P O G Q T X R D B L F D G G
D P Y P C F K U C L D W W C Z C I Z N U W M J D
U K F Y K E A M I V I O Y S C M C D J X E U M J
B P H R V K K K C C X S W D N G O Y L X W C H D
W J Q L S X O M U S C L E J A D I H S Z E O F Y
P V N E D N D J X B M M Y U V A D D I Q B S C K
R X R S M Q J J P M T L Y R S A X A M Q N A K Z
A R O T C T G S N B D E F O L A E M D S W S B Y
P E P M E B K L Z E V U J S P F U U T E T J F E
```

Muscle	Arytenoid	Cricoid
Tilt	Pitch	Cells
Ciliated	Ventricle	Phonation
Vocal	Ligament	Glottis
Vocalis	Epithelium	Mucosa
Vocal Fold	Reinke's	Bernoulli

Section IV The larynx: the full picture

Putting it all together

In the previous three sections, we looked at the larynx both structurally and functionally. We have explored the overall shape and the individual parts of the vocal tract, we have looked at all the muscles contained within that structure and how they work together.

We have also investigated the vocal folds and seen how they are manipulated by the intrinsic muscles of the larynx to create sound and explored the extrinsic muscles of the larynx in order to understand their part in supporting the mechanism.

This section puts this knowledge together to show how a clearer understanding of the anatomy and physiology of the larynx can be practically applied to the act of singing. As a result, this is more complicated than previous sections and there is still much that is not fully understood. Greater knowledge and understanding of the instrument is constantly emerging and we have noted this possibility at a couple of key places in the book.

For some of the most contentious subjects covered in this section, such as phonatory qualities, for example, we have drawn together views from a cross-section of pedagogical viewpoints as well as our own, to ensure we give as generous a definition as possible. Overall, this section of *The Singer's Guide to the Larynx* is what could be described as a courageous attempt to define some of the more confusing terms used - often without clarity - within the singing profession.

In Section IV we are maintaining a strict focus on those aspects of sound production, such as timbre, harmonics, vibrato, register and the different types of sound that originate **primarily** in the larynx. A discussion of the resonance qualities of the entire vocal tract, for example, which contribute significantly to the production of sound, lie outside the scope of this larynx-centred workbook.

A shortlist of recommended reading completes this last section of the book.

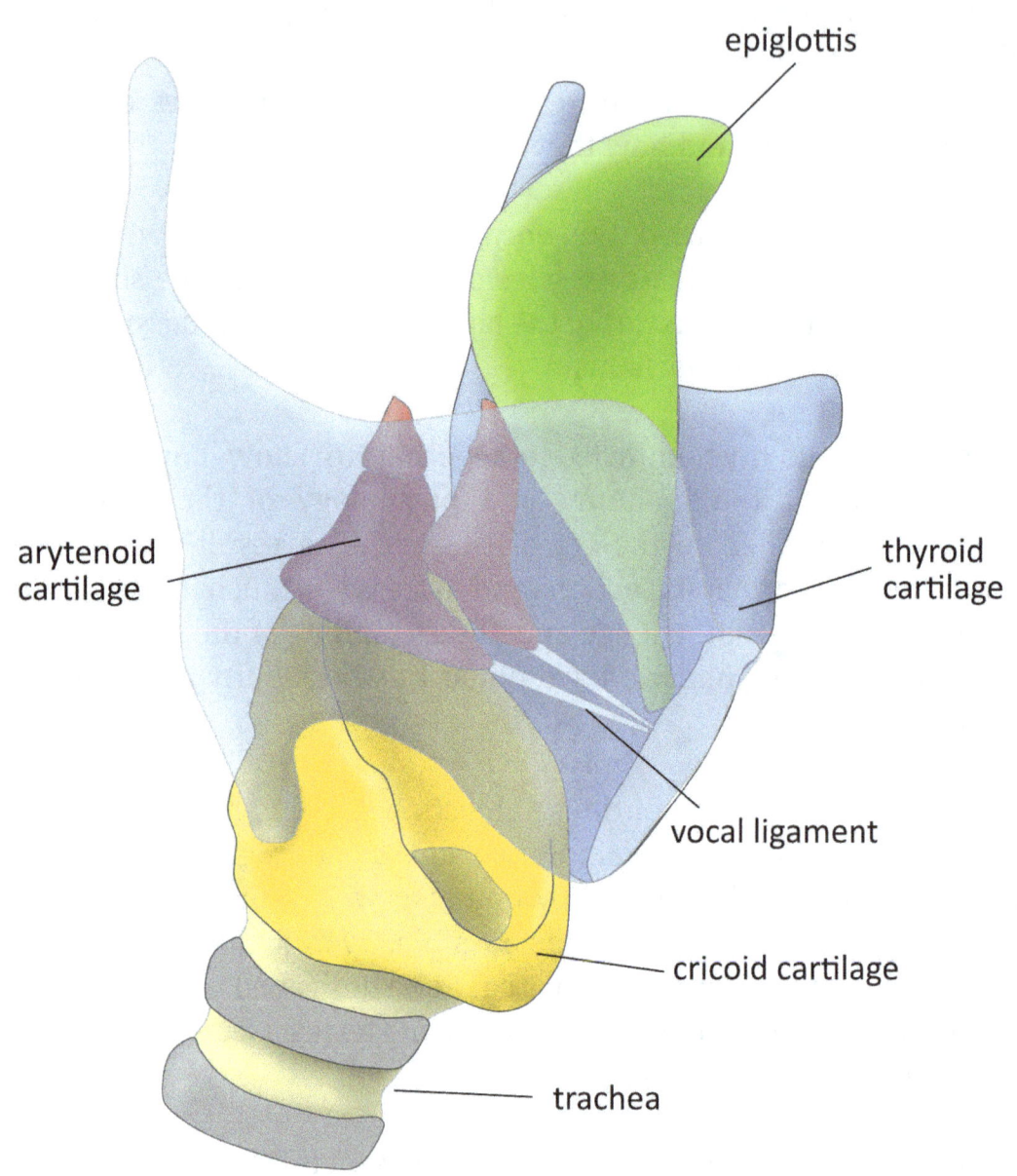

Side view of the larynx

The larynx and the singing voice

The larynx is **the source of sound**. It is not, however, the only component in the complex instrument that forms the singing voice. The sound, although generated by the larynx, is powered from the lungs, resonated in the vocal tract, and shaped and articulated in the pharynx and oral cavity. The larynx is only part of the whole vocal picture, but it is very important because:

1. It regulates **pitch**
2. It contributes to **timbre**
3. It affects the quality of **resonance**
    a. Through its own resonant cavity (i.e. the space within the larynx above the vocal folds, which is known as the vestibule).
    b. Through its position, which determines the length of the vocal tract. If the larynx is low the vocal tract will be longer; If it is high, the vocal tract will be shorter.

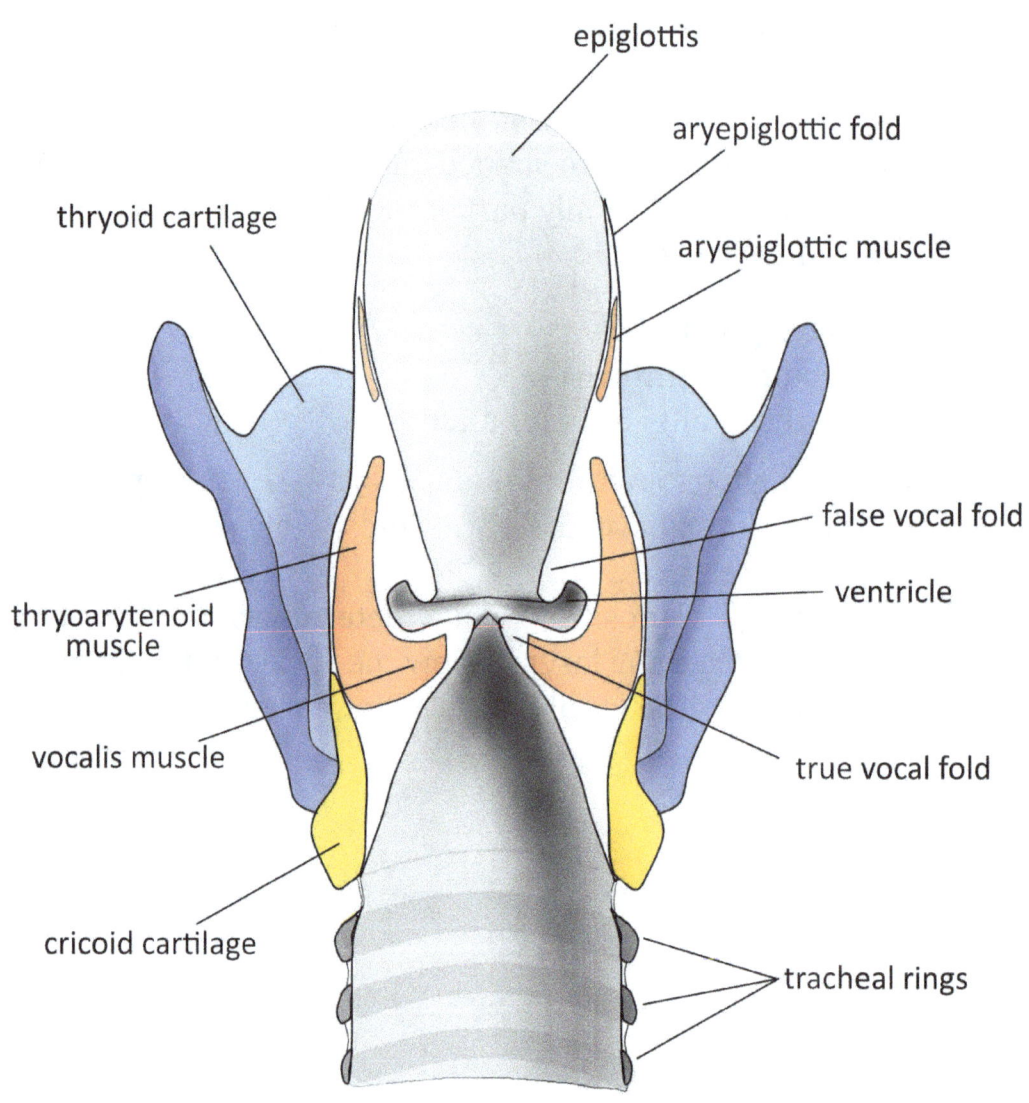

Coronal section through the larynx seen from behind

The internal shape of the larynx

This is a tube that extends upwards from the tracheal rings to the epiglottis. Its shape is modified by the structures within it.

There are two separate spaces within the larynx: the space above the vocal folds is known as the **vestibule**, and the space below the vocal folds is known as the **subglottic space.**

The whole of the internal structure of the larynx is covered with epithelium.

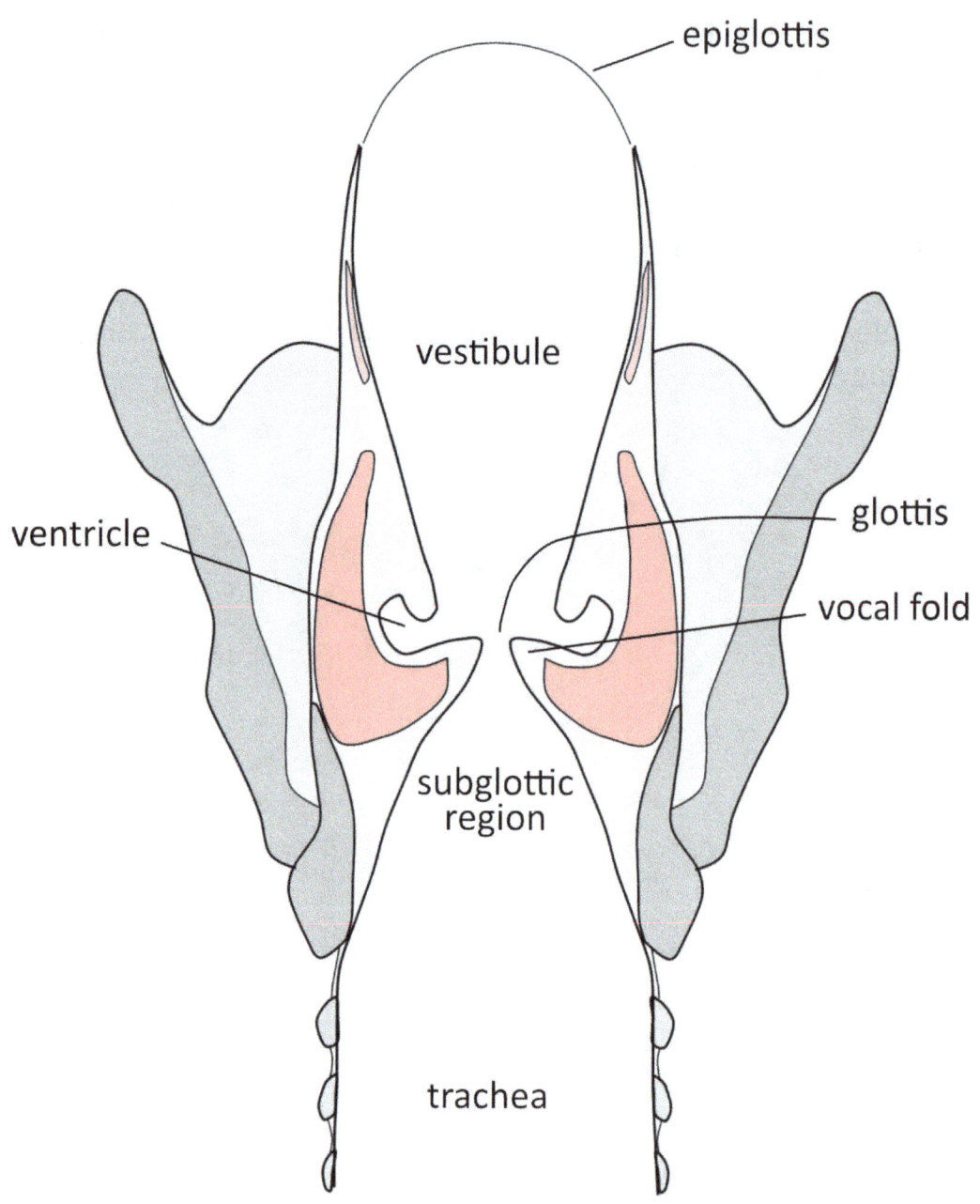

Coronal view of the larynx from behind to show its internal spaces

Inside the larynx

From the bottom of the interior of the larynx to the top, the following are found:

1. The **subglottic space**
   The subglottic space lies immediately beneath the vocal folds. When the folds are closed, the air pressure builds up beneath them until it is sufficient to push them apart and initiate the process that generates sound.

2. The **vocal folds** and the **glottis**
   The vocal folds form the floor of the resonating chamber within the larynx and set up the vibrations in the air flow. The **glottis** is the space between the vocal folds. It closes for phonation.

3. **The ventricles**
   Two narrow chambers that extend horizontally from the vestibule which is situated immediately above the true vocal folds. Their contribution to resonance within the vocal tract is still unknown.

4. **The false vocal folds** Also known as the **vestibular folds**, the false vocal folds contain many mucus-secreting cells and glands that lubricate the true vocal folds. Although not generally used in singing, there are certain extreme forms of vocalisation, such as 'growling' where the false vocal folds are pressed against the true folds to create a low frequency vibration. This action is also found in throat singing where it creates a constant low drone whose harmonics are then picked out to create the melody.

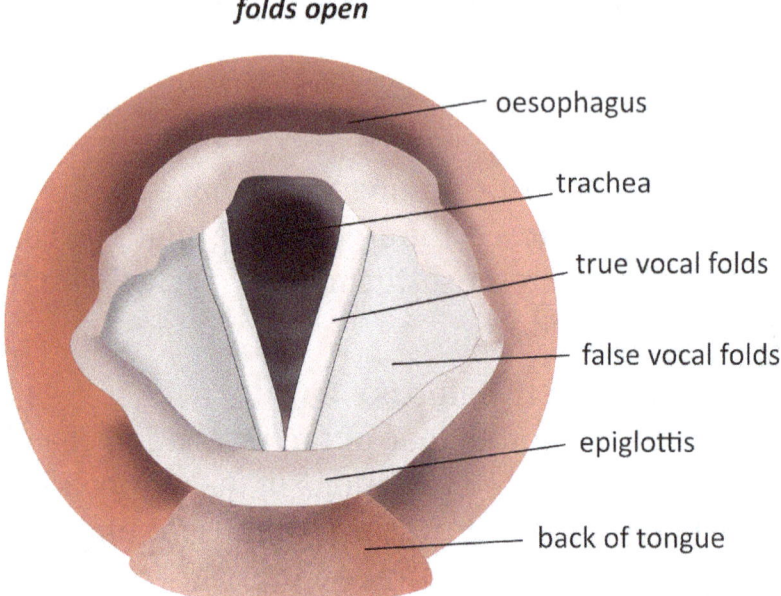
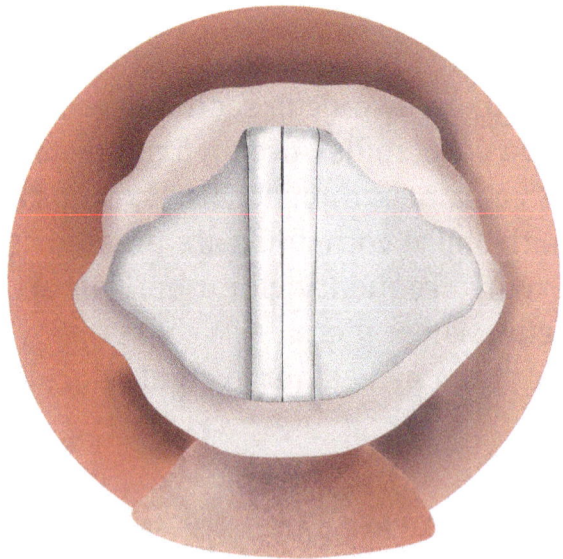

Glottis viewed from above to show true and false vocal folds in open and closed position

5. **The vestibule**
   This resonating space extends upwards from the vocal folds to the epiglottis. At the top of the vestibule are the aryepiglottic muscles. It has been suggested that they can narrow the upper opening of the vestibule, thus altering the resonance of the chamber. However, doubt has been cast on this as the aryepiglottic muscles are poorly developed[1] and some believe that vestibular narrowing is mainly achieved by the action of the middle pharyngeal constrictor muscle and the backward movement of the tongue pressing down on the epiglottis[2,3,4].

---

[1] Reidenbach, M.M. (1998) Aryepglottic fold: normal topography and clinical implications. *Clinical Anatomy* 11:223–35
[2] Obert K., Personal communication.
[3] Vandaele, D.J., Perlman, A.L. and Cassell, M.D. (1995) Intrinsic fibre architecture and attachments of the human epiglottis and their contributions to the mechanism of deglutition. *Journal of Anatomy* 186(Pt 1):1–15.
[4] Titze, I. and Verdolini Abbott, K. (2012). *Vocology*. Utah: National Centre for Voice and Speech, pp. 298–9.

The mucosal epithelium

A thin lining that covers the entire vocal tract from the inside of the nose to the lungs with the one exception of the free edges of the vocal folds, which is covered with squamous epithelium. The mucosal epithelium is made up of a layer of cells of different types.
There are two main types of cell within the mucosal epithelium:

    1. Those that **secrete mucus** (goblet cells)

    2. Those that **move the mucus out of the larynx** upwards (ciliated cells)

There are also glands within the larynx for secreting watery fluid and mucus. The watery fluid is thinner than mucus and keeps the tract moist. Mucus is a thick substance that traps dust, allergens, bacteria and other particles so that they do not pass into the lungs (see section III).

Note: Around 1.5 to 2 litres of mucosal secretions are swallowed every day.

The mucosal epithelium and singing

When the vocal tract is irritated or infected, the mucus becomes thicker. This will have an adverse effect on the voice.

Certain foods may also increase mucus in the vocal tract or cause it to thicken. The most common of these are chocolate and dairy products, although increased mucus can also be a result of food allergies. Caffeine-based drinks may thicken mucus due to their dehydrating effect, so a good regular intake of water is essential.

Excessive mucus production may also occur, as a protective mechanism when acid reflux from the stomach irritates the vocal folds. Then, mucus will collect around the vocal folds and impede their movement. This will have a negative impact on sound production and may also lead to excessive throat clearing, where, to dislodge the mucus, the folds are pressed together very strongly to force the air through them. This repeated action can damage the edges of the vocal folds.

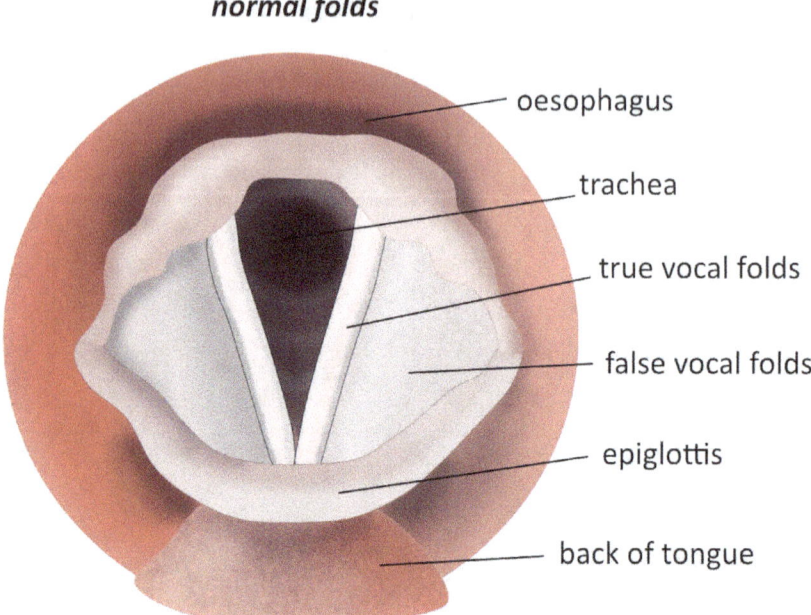

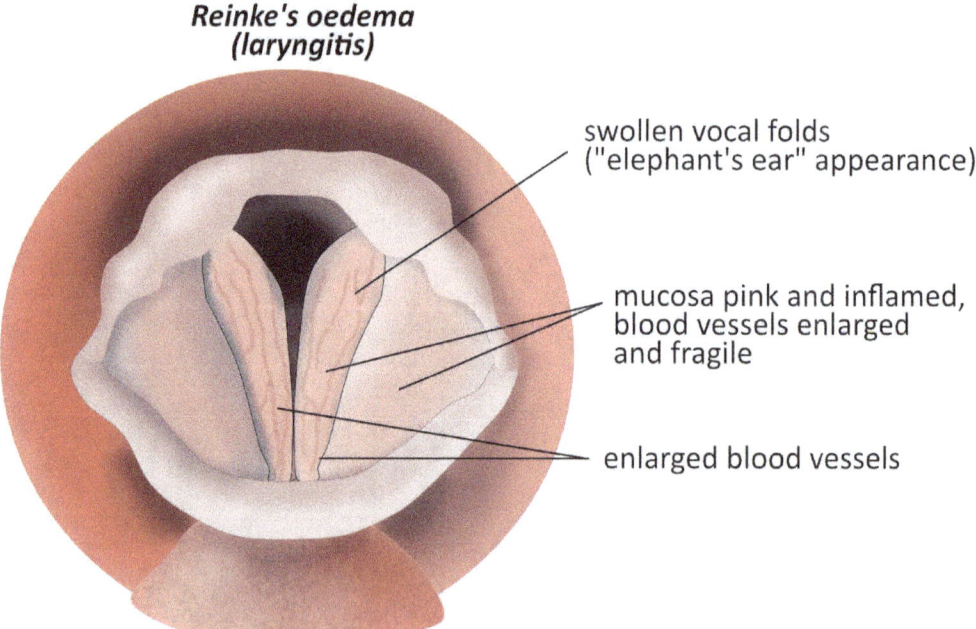

Effects of Reinke's oedema

Reinke's space

The epithelium that covers the vocal folds is attached by thin fibres to the underlying **vocalis** muscle to create a layer known as **Reinke's space**. During infection, repeated harsh singing or as a side-effect of smoking or acid reflux, the space may become engorged with fluid and cause swelling of the vocal folds. This is known as **Reinke's oedema**.

A rough, hoarse voice, loss of range and power and persistent vocal fatigue are common symptoms of many voice disorders such as Reinke's oedema and should be investigated by a specialist.

The creation of sound

1. The pressure of air from beneath the glottis pushes apart the vocal folds.
2. These open and close continually during the breath, resulting in pulsations in the airflow that are perceived as sound.
3. The rate of opening and closing is determined by how much the folds are stretched lengthways. Broadly speaking, the greater the stretch, the higher the pitch, although the amount of tension in the vocalis muscles, which changes the vibrating mass of the folds, is also a factor.
4. As the folds are pushed apart by the pressure of the breath, the speed of air coming up from beneath them is increased.
5. This causes the pressure between the folds to fall (Bernoulli Effect).
6. Because of the falling pressure and the elasticity of the stretched folds, the glottis closes.
7. The cycle then repeats.

Note: the first opening and closing of the vocal folds initiates the onset of the note and the cycle of vocal fold movement maintains it. The last note of a sung phrase is completed by stopping the vocal fold movement cleanly. This ends the sound.

This is a simplified account of the mechanisms underlying the opening and closing of the vocal folds. Pressure changes above the folds also contribute to fold opening and closure in a process called *inertive reactance*. Such a topic is beyond the scope of this book but a fuller description of this and other contributing factors can be found here:

> Titze I.R. (2008) The human instrument. *Scientific American* **298**(1):78–85.
> Titze I.R. and Verdolini Abbott K. (2012) *Vocology: The science and practice of voice rehabilitation*. Salt Lake City, UT: National Center for Voice & Speech. pp290-1.

It is often believed that the intrinsic muscles of the larynx contract at the same frequency as the sung note. This is not the case because it is impossible for these muscles to contract at such high frequencies. Instead, they maintain a constant tension in the folds and it is this tension that determines the rate of vibration in the airstream and therefore the frequency of the note.

Aspects of sound: pitch

Definition: pitch is a complex property of sound, but here we simply define it as *how high or low the note is*. We are not talking about the subtleties of sound placement and tuning.

The pitch of the sound is determined by how many times the vocal folds open and close each second due to the flow of air between them.
For example:
> When singing a middle C (C4), the folds open and close at 261.6 times a second, or roughly, 262 Hertz (Hz).
> When singing the C above middle C (C5), the vocal folds will open and close at around 523 Hz.
> When singing a top C (C6, or two octaves above middle C), this will increase to around 1046 Hz.

Note that with every increasing octave there is a doubling of frequency. In singing, pitch is determined by the **degree of tension** in the vocal folds. This is increased by the contraction of the **cricothyroid muscles**.

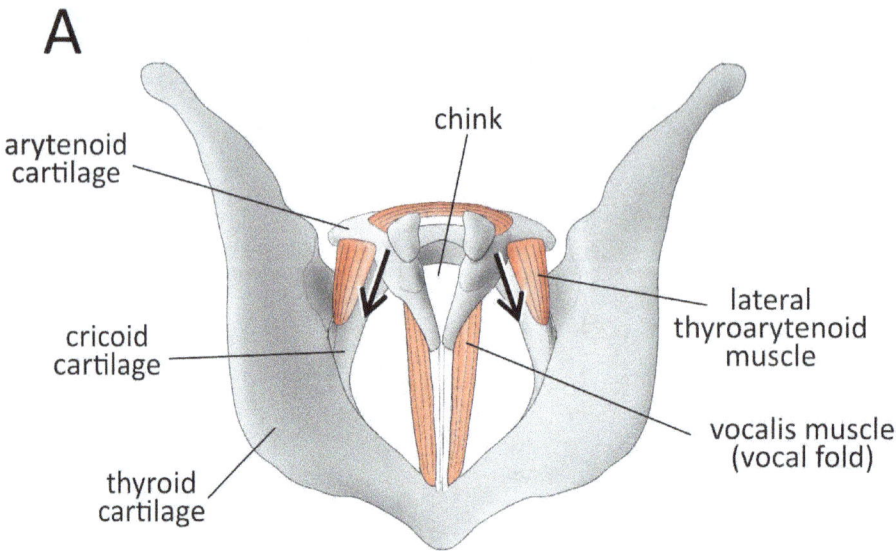

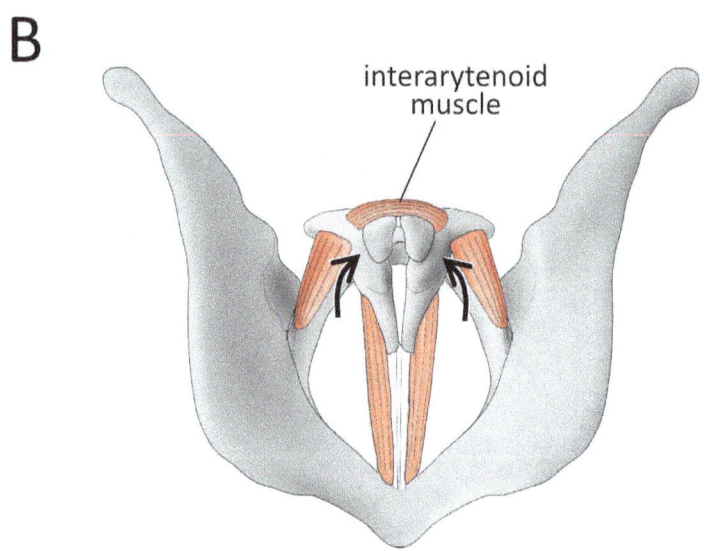

The action of the interarytenoid muscles during stretching of the folds

A. As the vocal folds are stretched by the action of the cricothyroid muscles, the arytenoid cartilages are drawn forwards. This may create a gap or 'chink' at the back of the glottis which is prevented by the action of the interarytenoid muscles.

B. The interarytenoid muscles are shown closing the gap at the back of the vocal folds.

Stretching of the vocal folds

The stretching of the folds is achieved through the backwards movement of the **arytenoid cartilages**. This is brought about by the action of the cricothyroid muscles which bring the front edges of the cricoid and thyroid cartilages together. In the singing world, opinion is still divided as to whether it is the cricoid or thyroid cartilage that moves, or whether this action might vary between individuals, voice types and vocal styles.

Note: Classical singing teachers have generally taught that it is the thyroid cartilage that tilts downwards as pitch increases. While other schools of vocal pedagogy may assert a different action, the only current scientific evidence, based on medical imaging of the larynx during singing has shown a backward tilting of the cricoid cartilage.[1] We do know, however, that any action of these cartilages is initiated **by the singing task.** They are not consciously activated by the singer.

Stretching of vocal folds can cause the arytenoid cartilages to slide forwards. This may leave a gap or 'chink' at the back of the glottis through which air can escape, resulting in a breathy sound. The 'chink' may not appear in some circumstances depending on the type of vocal sound being produced. If the interarytenoid muscles are active at the same time as the cricothyroid muscles, the glottic closure will be more complete during phonation and the 'chink' will not develop when the folds are stretched. In young singers and during female adolescence for example, a breathy sound is common and natural. This will gradually disappear as the voice changes and develops.

Higher pitches: Although the above actions explain the regulation of pitch in the standard vocal ranges, they do not fully explain the mechanisms involved in reaching the extremely high notes e.g. flute/whistle register.

One theory[2], is that once the folds have been stretched to their maximum, the pitch is raised further through the restriction of the length of the vibrating parts of the folds.

---

[1]Unteregger F., *et al* (2017) 3D analysis of the movements of the laryngeal cartilages during singing *Laryngoscope* **127**(7):1639–43.

[2] Titze I.R. and Hunter E.J. (2004) Normal vibration frequencies of the vocal ligament. *Journal of the Acoustical Society of America* **115**(5):2264–9.

The slackening (reducing tension) of the vocal folds

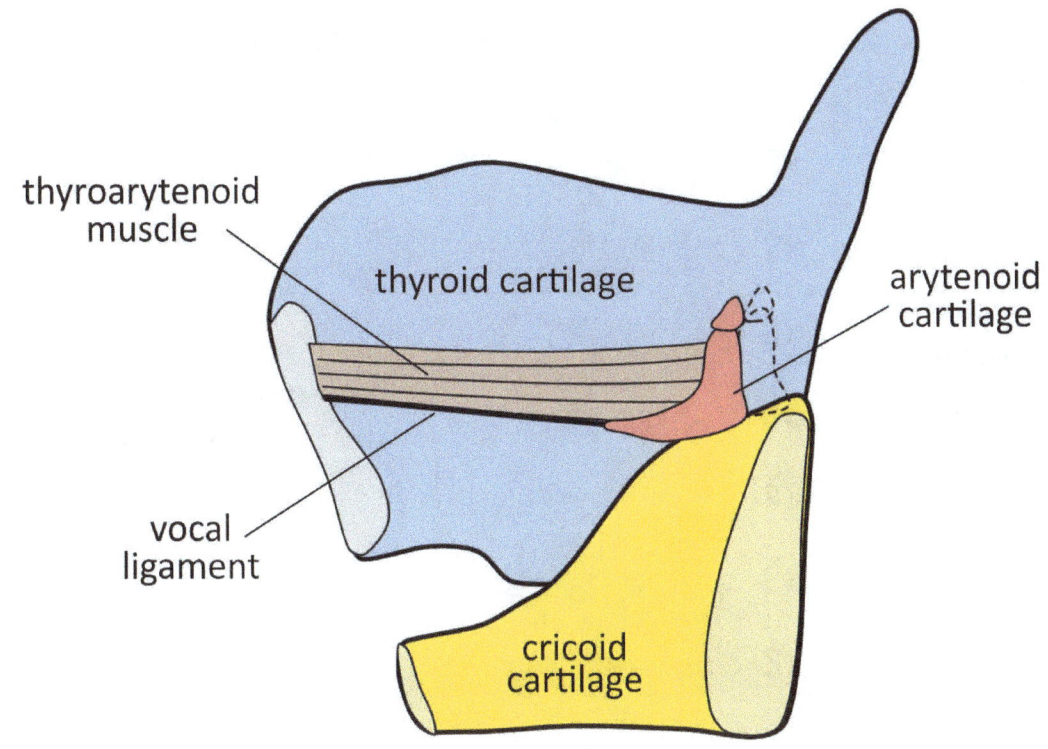

The inside of the larynx as if it was cut in half

When the thyroarytenoid muscle contracts, it pulls the arytenoid cartilages forwards from their original position (dashed outline). The vocal folds then slacken (the tension is reduced) and the pitch of the note falls.

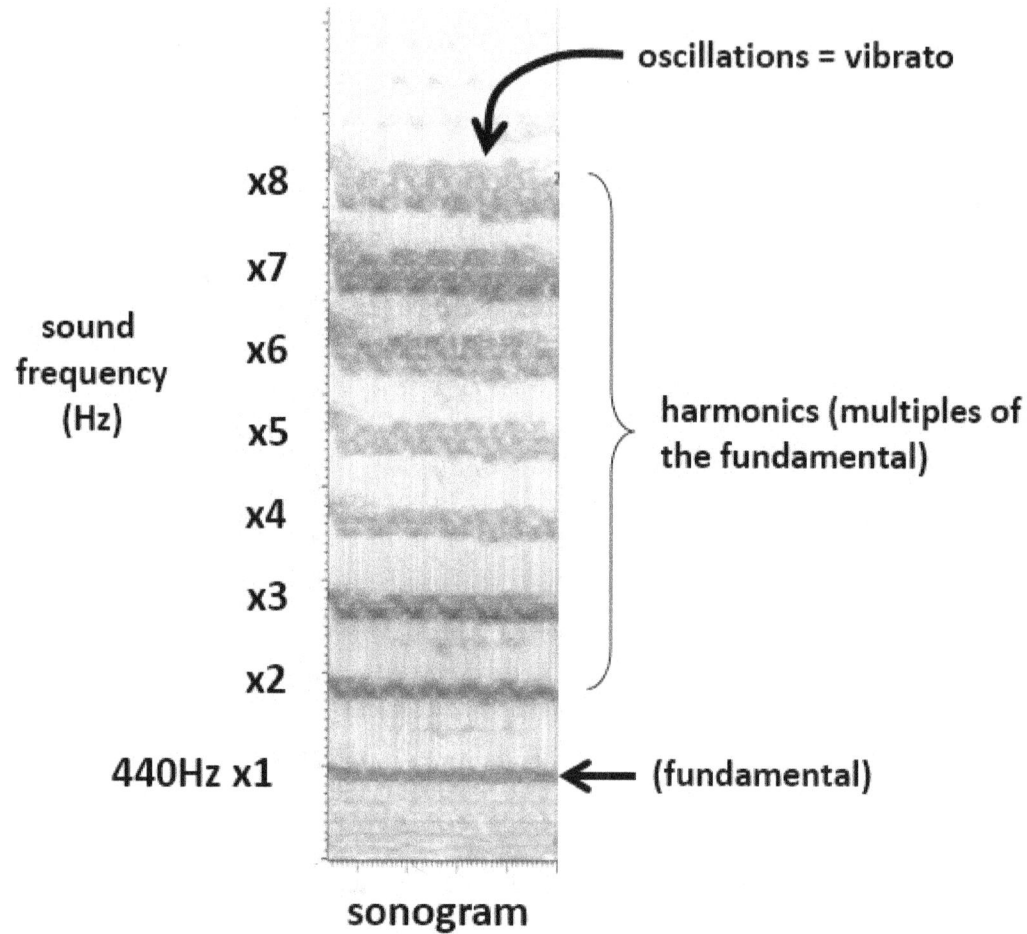

Sonogram showing the harmonics of A (440Hz) sung by a mezzo-soprano. The fundamental is the perceived frequency of the sung note. The harmonics are multiples of this frequency.

Harmonics

A sung note contains, not one, but many frequencies (Hz) which form a **harmonic series**.

The frequency of each harmonic is a multiple of the lowest harmonic in each series which represents the pitch of the note. When middle C (261.6 Hz) is sung, for example, the second harmonic is twice this frequency (523.2 Hz), the third harmonic is three times this frequency: (784.8 Hz) and so on.

This harmonic series is generated in the larynx, but the relative strengths of the different harmonics can be adjusted by the resonance qualities of the vocal tract. These qualities will be determined by the position of the larynx within the neck, the width of the throat, the shape and position of the tongue and lips.

Such manipulation of harmonics brings about change in the quality of the sound, such as vocal colour, brightness of tone and differing vowel sounds and can also be used to enhance loudness and to create the singer's formant, a strong vocal tract resonance centred around 3000 Hz which will help carry the voice over an entire orchestra. The demands of singing **at high** pitches require the modification of vowels and adjustments of jaw position.

Sources of further reading on this subject
Watson, A.H.D. (2009) *The biology of musical performance and performance-related Injury*. Lanham, MD: Scarecrow Press.
Titze I.R. and Verdolini Abbott K. (2012) *Vocology: The science and practice of voice rehabilitation*. Salt Lake City, UT: National Center for Voice & Speech.

Types of phonation in singing

Flow: If the folds are held gently together, a smooth sound as used in classical singing is generated. The airflow is ample and the vocal folds open and close together gently in the airstream.

Pressed: If the vocal folds are pressed strongly together it creates a harsher or more edgy sound that is used in some styles of contemporary singing as a vocal quality. Pressed phonation is achieved through the forceful action of the **interarytenoid** and the **lateral cricoarytenoid muscles**.

This may be accompanied by an inward movement of the vestibular or false vocal folds[1]. Note: Inexperienced singers may use pressed phonation inappropriately to achieve volume, running the risk of hoarseness or more sustained damage to the edges of the vocal folds due to the force with which they collide.

Breathy: Although most of the sound is created by the movement of the vocal folds, in breathy phonation the airflow is increased, the onset is aspirated and some air escapes through a small 'chink' between the arytenoid cartilages. Breathy singing is a feature of some vocal styles, particularly jazz, and can also be used as an interpretative effect within a song.

Whisper: The vocal folds are partly open at the back, allowing the air to pass through this gap without moving the main body of the folds. The folds do not vibrate. In addition to this, the false vocal folds are brought closer together. **Whisper is generally related to speech**: Instead of a voiced sound, a hissing sound is created due to the turbulence of air passing through the gap. Vowels and consonants are articulated in the usual way but are unvoiced. If the airflow is too turbulent, as in sustained speech, for example, or during infection, this can dry the moist surface of the vocal folds and put strain on the voice.

[1]Cooke, A., *et al.* (1997) Characteristics of vocal fold adduction related to voice onset *Journal of Voice* **11**(1):12–22

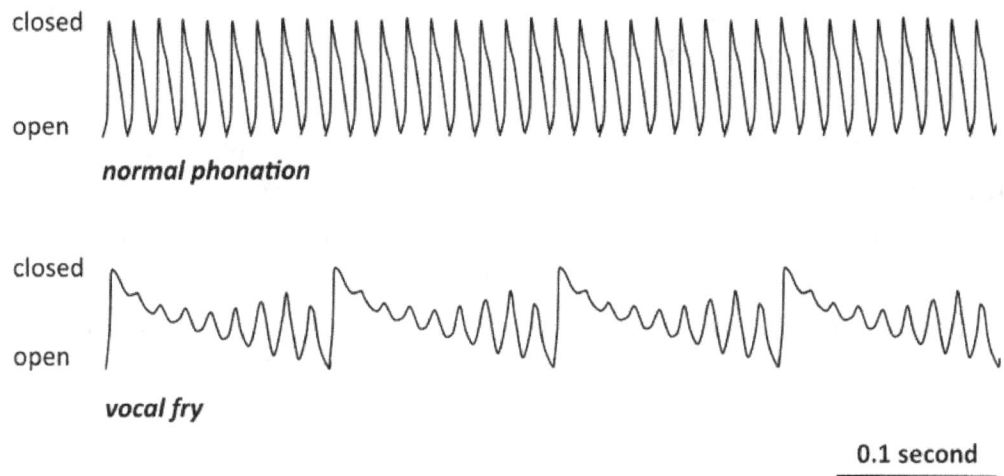

Pattern of vocal fold movement with and without 'vocal fry'.

The pattern of the opening and closing of the glottis when singing the C below middle C is represented in the top trace. This is compared with the same note sung with vocal fry in the bottom trace. Note that every tenth peak is larger than the rest. These peaks represent the pulses in the vocal fry.

Vocal fry/creak: occurs low in the range – in both speaking and singing when the vocal folds are slack and thick but held firmly together. As with other forms of singing, the folds open and close at the frequency of the sung note. The 'fry' is a series of separate pulses at a lower frequency that can be heard superimposed on the sound. It has been described both as a vocal quality and as a register.

Twang: this is a bright sound with a strongly perceived nasal quality and forward tone that is associated, particularly in the U.S. with the style of Country and Western singing. In the U.K. it is also described as a vocal quality that can be used in other styles of singing such as musical theatre, or perhaps as a 'mix' into a higher register. The higher harmonics of twanged notes are more intense.

In twang, the vocal folds are held together firmly and an intense resonating space is created immediately above them by a narrowing of the upper opening of the vestibule. This narrowing may be caused by the contraction of the aryepiglottic muscle in conjunction with the back of the tongue, and through the action of the middle pharyngeal constrictor.

Belt: Commonly used, for example, in pop and musical theatre styles of singing, this sound is strong and emotional in effect. Belting is chest register or speech quality dominant, often bright, loud and 'forward' in tone, *but not always*.

Belting styles have recently been divided by some schools of pedagogy into various sub-categories such as heavy belt, nasal belt, twangy belt, brassy belt, etc, but such sub-definitions are by no means universal!

Many of the actions associated with belting are currently thought to happen outside the larynx, for example in the extrinsic muscles of the neck and in acoustic adjustments within the pharynx.

The 'belt' sound is the result of the interface of certain harmonics and formants. Our simple aim here is to show what is currently believed to happen within the larynx itself, where the following features have frequently been attributed to this style of singing.

The larynx is generally believed to be in a high position, although some professional singers belt very successfully with a low larynx. The vocal folds are pressed firmly together and the vocalis muscles remain contracted into higher pitches, keeping the vocal folds thickened. This results in a longer closed phase within the vocal fold cycle (see section III).

Note: vocal tract adjustments for 'belt' are still not fully understood and there is widespread disagreement among both vocal pedagogues and voice scientists as to what is happening within the larynx and how this sound is produced. The descriptions presented above represent a general overview drawn from various pedagogical viewpoints and discussions.

Notable papers for further reading

Sundberg J., Gramming P. and Lovetri J. (1993) Comparisons of pharynx, source, formant, and pressure characteristics in operatic and musical theatre singing. *Journal of Voice* **7**(4):301–10.

Sundberg J., Thalen M. and Popeil L. (2012) Substyles of belting: phonatory and resonatory characteristics. *Journal of Voice* **26**(1):44–50.

Popeil L.S. (1999) Comparing belt and classical techniques uing MRI and video-fluoroscopy. *Jounal of Singing* **56**(2):27–9.

Henrich N. (2006) Mirroring the voice from Garcia to the present day: some insights into singing voice registers. Logopedics Phoniatrics Vocology **31**(1):3–14.

Lebowitz A. and Baken R.J. (2011) Correlates of the belt voice: a broader examination. *Journal of Voice* **25**(2):159–65.

LoVetri, J. (2002) Contemporary Commercial Music: more than one way to use the vocal tract. *Journal of Singing* **58**(Jan/Feb):249–52

LoVetri, J. (2003) Female chest voice. *Journal of Singing* **60**(2):161–4.

Titze I. (2007) Belting and a high larynx position. *Journal of Singing* (May/June):557–8.

Echternach M., *et al.* (2014) Vocal tract shapes in different singing functions used in musical theater singing-a pilot study. *Journal of Voice* **28**(5):653 e651–653 e657.

Caffier P.P., *et al.* (2017) Common vocal effects and partial glottal vibration in professional nonclassical singers. *Journal of Voice* **32**(3):340–6.

Hirano M. (1988) Vocal mechanisms in singing: Laryngological and phoniatric aspects. *Journal of Voice* **2**(1):51–69.

LeBorgne, W.D., Lee, L., *et al.* (2010) Perceptual findings on the Broadway belt voice. *Journal of Voice* **24**(6):678–89

Timbre

Timbre is the quality of sound of a voice: whether it is bright, dark, rich or shrill. This can vary between voices, registers, and vowel quality.

The timbre of a voice is unique and can make a person's sound instantly recognisable. This is partly due to resonances within the vocal tract and how this affects the relative strengths of the harmonics of the sound generated in the larynx. Some aspects of timbre, however, are controlled solely by the larynx. These are the aspects we are concerned with here. Timbre is partly controlled by the action of the **vocalis muscles**:

1. If the vocalis muscles are relaxed, only the vocal ligaments and overlying epithelium vibrate and the sound is perceived as being brighter in timbre.
2. If the vocalis muscles are contracted then the whole mass of the vocal folds vibrates making the timbre appear richer and darker.

The **degree of contraction** of the **vocalis muscles** contributes to the sound quality of different vocal registers. To create a smooth transition between registers in the classical voice – in other words to effectively navigate the passaggi – the degree of contraction in the vocalis muscles must be changed gradually by 'mixing' the sound quality into the next register. This must commence before the register break. Techniques for achieving register shifts will vary between different styles of singing. Effects such as yodelling, for example, can deliberately accentuate the register break.

Registers

This is a contentious subject where unclear definitions abound, several terms are used interchangeably and there is a general lack of scientific evidence to fully explain the phenomenon of registration in the singing voice.

Here, we define registers as:

> Distinctly separate parts of the vocal range, each with their own timbre and quality that are separated by abrupt *shifts* or breaks. Every register is the result of a consistent pattern of vibration of the vocal folds. Every register *shift* is the result of a transition from one pattern of laryngeal muscle activity to the next.

In her book *Singing and Science* (Compton Publishing, 2014), Callaghan defines *register* as follows:

> 'The term register refers to a range of pitch having a consistent timbre…Since the 1970s, registers have been recognised as the result of interactions between laryngeal and acoustical events, occurring at predictable frequencies in different voice types.'

In his ground-breaking book *Hints on Singing* (E. Ascherberg 1894), Manuel Garcia defined *register* as follows:

> 'A series of homogeneous sounds produced by one mechanism, differing essentially from another series of equally homogeneous sounds produced by another mechanism.'

Generally – and there is a wide variation in terminology, definition and number of registers – classical singers have historically described three distinct vocal registers: low, chest or modal register; middle or mixed register; and high, falsetto or head register.

Some pedagogues add another two registers to this list: fry, creak or pulse register (the lowest in the range); and whistle, flute or flageolet register at the super-top end of the voice.

Others might characterise the male voice as being made up of 'chest', 'head' and 'falsetto' registers, while some researchers and pedagogues assert that there are only two perceivable registers: the heavier modal or 'chest' register and the lighter 'head' register. On top of this, the descriptors 'head' and 'chest' voice were originally used as terms for resonance i.e. where the voice was *perceived* to resonate in the body, rather than to denote any physiological difference.

As singers move through their vocal range, different qualities of sound may be associated with each register with abrupt transitions between the registers that require navigation. Proficient singers can prepare and adjust for these transitions so that they can move between register shifts without any perceptible change in sound quality. This ability is the result of a good vocal technique
.

The registers of the lower regions of the voice are darker in timbre. This is because the **whole mass of the vocal folds vibrates**, including the **vocalis** muscles, which are **contracted.** In the higher regions of the voice the sound is brighter in timbre. This is because the **vocalis** muscle is **relaxed**, so that **only the vocal ligament vibrates**.

The falsetto register can be breathy or clear in quality. This may also be a matter of artistic and stylistic choice (see **Timbre**). It is also described as a vocal quality as well as a register.

When we sing even higher in the vocal range, such as the flute/ whistle register it is thought that only part of the length of the fold may vibrate, making the sound lighter still[1,2].

This is believed to be due to the contraction of just a short segment of the vocalis muscles while the rest of the folds remain static. This makes the vibrating section of the fold shorter than its entire length.

[1] Rubin H.J. and Hirt C.C. (1960) The falsetto. A high speed cinematographic study. *Laryngoscope* **70**:1305–24.
[2] Sanders I., et al. (1998) Muscle spindles are concentrated in the superior vocalis subcopartment of the human thyroarytenoid muscle *Journal of Voice* 12(1):7–16.

There is still a great deal to be learned about vocal registers. Information is patchy and understanding has been hampered by confused terminology.

Other main sources on registers

Callaghan J. (2014) *Singing and Science; body, brain and voice.* Oxford: Compton Publishing.

Hirano M. (1988) Vocal mechanisms in singing: Laryngological and phoniatric aspects *Journal of Voice* **2**(1):51–69.

Kochis-Jennings K.A., *et al.* (2014) Cricothyroid muscle and thyroarytenoid muscle dominance in vocal register control: preliminary results *Journal of Voice* **28**(5):652 e621–652 e629.

Miller R. (1986) *The structure of singing : system and art in vocal technique* New York, NY: Schirmer; London: Collier Macmillan.

Titze I. (1988) A framework for the study of vocal registers. *Journal of Voice* **2**(3):183–194.

Titze I.R. and Verdolini Abbott K. (2012) *Vocology: The science and practice of voice rehabilitation.* Salt Lake City, UT: National Center for Voice & Speech.

Vibrato

Vibrato is a fluctuation in both the pitch and intensity of the voice, generally at a frequency of around 5.5 -7Hz. In other words, the sound is oscillating rapidly around a central pitch. If the vibrato is too slow, the pitch may vary too widely and manifest as what is colloquially known among singers as a 'wobble'. If the vibrato is too fast, this could manifest itself as a 'bleat.'

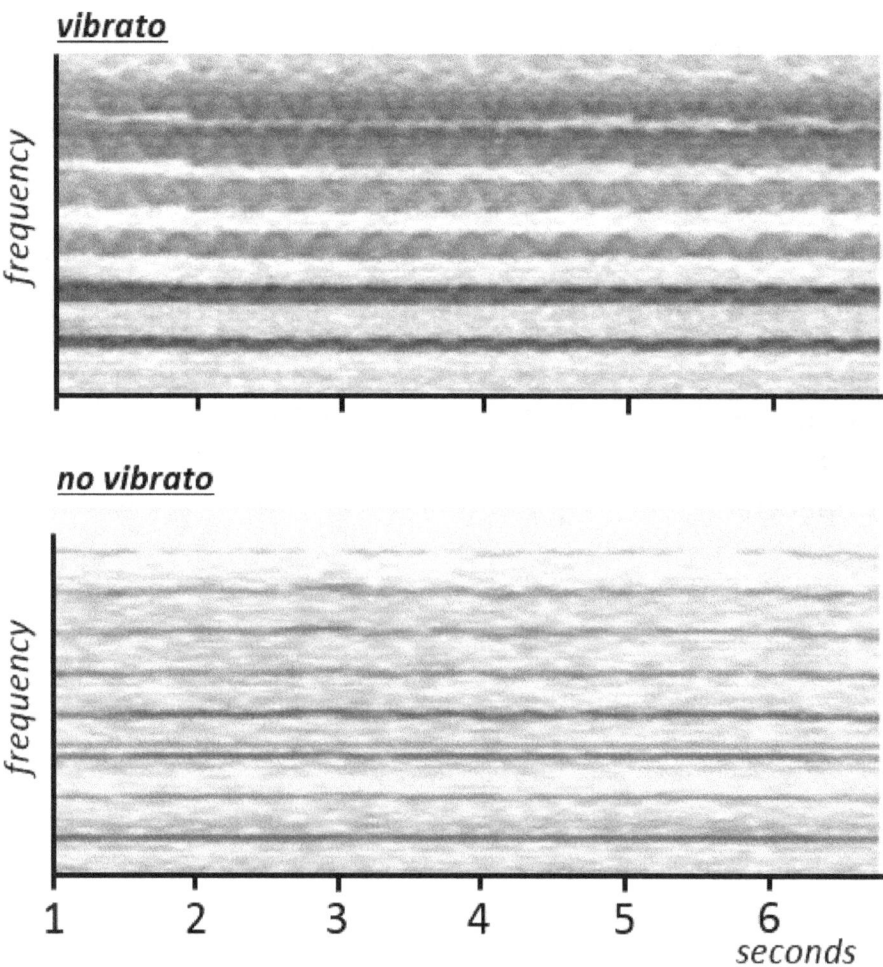

Sonogram traces of notes sung with and without vibrato. For the note with vibrato, fluctuations in frequency are clearly visible in the 3rd to 5th harmonics. The harmonics of the note sung without vibrato show very little fluctuation.

Classical singing: Vibrato is both intrinsic to the classical singing voice and highly individual. A good vibrato has a regular rate and is consistent around the pitch of the sung note at a magnitude of around 50 cents.

Sustained vibrato in classical singing is currently thought to arise mainly from fluctuations in the activity of several intrinsic laryngeal muscles:

Cricothyroid muscles
Thyroarytenoid muscles
Vocalis muscles
Lateral cricoarytenoid muscles

It can also involve similar patterns of activity in the extrinsic muscles that control the position of the larynx in the neck, such as the **sternothyroid** and **sternohyoid** muscles. This results in an oscillation in the height of the larynx which occurs in phase with the vibrato.
Other elements of the vocal tract outside the larynx may also oscillate with vibrato, such as the tongue, epiglottis, soft palate and pharyngeal wall. In some singers, fluctuations in the activity of several respiratory and abdominal muscles have been noted. (Watson, *et al.*, 2012).

In classical singing, a consistent stylistically acceptable vibrato is both desirable and required. In other contemporary styles of singing, such as musical theatre, jazz and pop, vibrato may be applied as a stylistic tool rather than a consistent element of the sound, particularly at the end of the sung phrase.

Two notable chapters on the subject of vibrato

Hirano M., Hibi S. and Hagino S. (1995) Physiological aspects of vibrato. In: Dejonckere P.H., Hirano M. and Sundberg J. (eds) *Vibrato* San Diego, CA: Singular Publishing pp. 9–32.

Sundberg J. (1999) The perception of singing. VI Vibrato. In: Deutsch D. (ed) *The Psychology of Music* 2ed. San Diego, CA: Academic Press. pp. 171–214.

Revision questionnaire

1. Describe the internal shape of the larynx.
2. Name one of the two main spaces within the larynx.
3. What are the ventricles?
4. Name a muscle that lies at the opening of the vestibule?
5. Give six points to describe the stages in the creation of sound.
6. Define the term 'Hertz.'
7. What is vibrato?
8. Which muscles are responsible for creating vibrato?
9. What is a *register*?
10. Which changes in muscular activity are involved in transitioning the first passaggio?
11. What does *harmonic series* mean?
12. Which muscles are involved in closing the 'chink' at the back of the vocal folds?
13. Which muscles slacken the vocal folds?
14. Give a definition of 'timbre'.
15. Which muscles control timbre?
16. Which muscles are responsible for pressed phonation?
17. What is flow phonation?
18. What is the importance of formants in singing?
19. What is vocal fry or creak?

Answers
1. Subglottic space 2. Ventricles 3. Vestibule 4. Epithelium 5. Mucus 6. Oedema 7. Reinke's Space 8. Hertz 9. Cricothyroid muscles 10. Harmonics 11. Formant 12. Timbre 13. Phonation

Colour and name the parts

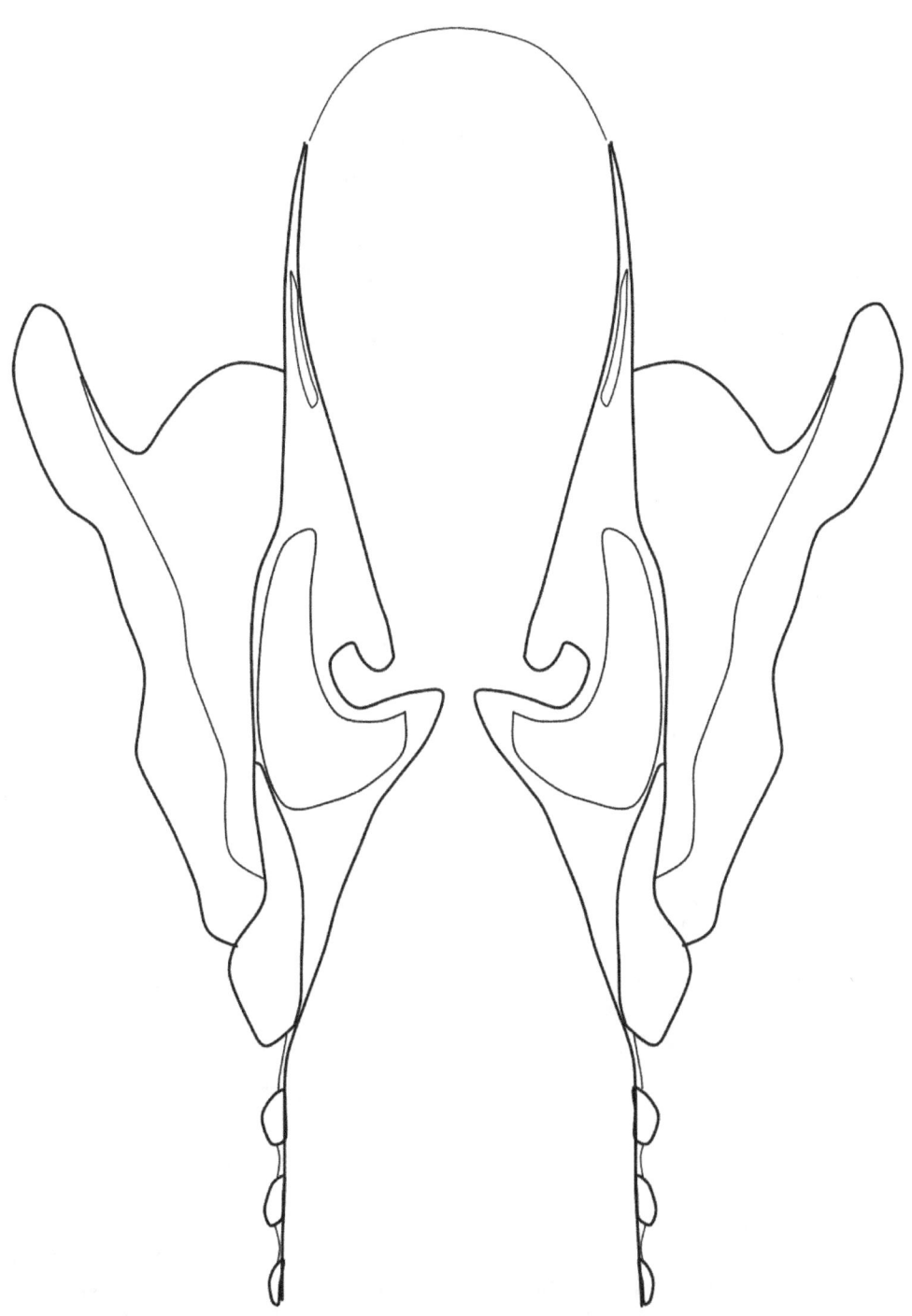

Word matching

Draw lines to pair the correct anatomical terms related to laryngeal anatomy and singing

Reinke's	Harmonic
Pressed	Phonation
Inter-	Bernoulli
Formant	Arytenoids
Projection	Glottic
Series	Singer's
Arytenoids	Epithelial
Effect	Vocal
Sub-	Oedema
Mucosa	Ary-
Epiglottic	Inter-

Answers

1. Subglottic space 2. Ventricles 3. Vestibule 4. Epithelium 5. Mucus 6. Oedema 7. Reinke's Space 8. Hertz 9. Cricothyroid muscles 10. Harmonics 11. Formant 12. Timbre 13. Phonation

Word scramble

Unscramble the following terms

1. OBUACGTTLSECIPS _____

2. SECRTEILVN _____

3. EBTVISUEL _____

4. ILUEPHMITE _____

5. SMCUU _____

6. DEMAEO _____

7. KCANRESPSEIE _____

8. ZRTEH _____

9. ULHOCSOTDRMYECIRSCI _____

10. HRSOINMCA _____

11. ANROTMSF _____

12. RBIETM _____

13. NONOIPTAH _____

Answers

1. Subglottic space 2. Ventricles 3. Vestibule 4. Epithelium 5. Mucus 6. Oedema 7. Reinke's Space 8. Hertz 9. Cricothyroid muscles 10. Harmonics 11. Formants 12. Timbre 13. Phonation

```
N G P V B F Y L J Q P M S Z R D S Y P X G A N H
S H A R M O N I C S Y P G H X P Z V L N X H J E
I S Q P J G U Q O G W Z L M T U X O I Y K B W D
D F S L N W A B P L N K D I J W K C S R E H S I
L U O A I R S T R E A M Z D V B W A D A R H I O
O P J I N C K S G S I T T O L G M L E L B I H N
F J P J Y A H V R K I E W P C T T I K C M Z Z E
L V K Y L M N T U D U V L Q W D P S R R I W F T
A M Q A M A X Y J E A S D R P B N W U H T W T Y
C U I U G P D R B S A U H K J A O I P R S F K R
O I S Q V K P J O L N C Y S P Z I P K M X E Z A
V L K P Z L O A U I G U V H A E T O T C A S F O
U E Q N S Z S E I T Q M I G K S A A U Y F R C R
E H A V Z L S F L N Y H L G H W N S M C X A L Y
M T R R W F F V C A V C V D W J O W N L P O V H
B I Q D S A Y Y E M I T E I C W H U J E P H R T
D P A O K I N X S R B I A C Y M P T M J Y C N E
I E M R O V O G T O R P Z R H M D V Y N E I Y P
W A A G H L I P R F A D I N T P E D S V W X D D
D C B D A L S C M O T V D Z O I S Y M K U Z D S
V R X V V Q N Z B F I N Z F N S S C Y R J V C W
Q M K G H B E W M F O S Y S X S E S A L I H W R
N P J Q F S T K E L N Z R X Z N R C D V M Z N L
R E I N K E S S P A C E H C R Z P Q Q W F B X
```

Mucus	epithelium	Reinke's space
airstream	glottis	cycle
tension	pitch	thyroarytenoid
harmonics	formant	vibration
larynx	vocalis	timbre
hoarse	pressed phonation	vocal fold

Shortlist of further reading for singers

Calais-Germain B. and Germain F. (2016) *Anatomy of voice: how to enhance and project your best voice* Rochester, VT: Healing Arts Press.
Callaghan J. (2014) *Singing and science; body, brain and voice* Oxford: Compton Publishing.
Chapman J.L. (2006) *Singing and teaching singing: a holistic approach to classical voice.* San Diego, CA: Plural Publishing.
Davies D.G. and Jahn A.F. (2004) *Care of the professional voice* London: A & C Black.
Dayme M.B. (2005) *The performer's voice : realizing your vocal potential* New York, NY and London: WW Norton.
Dayme M.B. and Besterman A. (2009) *Dynamics of the singing voice* Vienna and London: Springer.
Fisher J.A. and Kayes G. (2018) *This is a voice: 99 exercises to train, project and harness the power of your voice* Presteigne: Vocal Process
Garcia M. (1894, 2015 classic reprint). *Hints on singing.* South Yarra, Victoria: Leopold Classic Library.
Gates R., Forrest L.A. and Obert K. (2013) *The owner's manual to the voice: a guide for singers and other professional voice users.* Oxford and New York, NY: Oxford University Press.
Harris T. and Howard D.M. (2018) *The voice clinic handbook* 2ed. Oxford: Compton Publishing.
Kayes G. (2017) *Singing and the actor*. London: Bloomsbury
McKinney J.C. (1982) *The diagnosis and correction of vocal faults* Nashville, TN: Broadman Press.
Miller R. (1986) The structure of singing: system and art in vocal technique. New York, NY: Schirmer; London: Collier Macmillan.
Potter, J. (ed). (2011) *Cambridge companion to singing.* Cambridge; Cambridge University Press.
Rubin J.S., Sataloff R.T. and Korovin G.S. (2006) *Diagnosis and treatment of voice disorders.* San Diego, CA: Plural Publishing.
Stark J.A. (1999) *Bel canto: a history of vocal pedagogy* Toronto: University of Toronto Press.
Sataloff R.T. (2006) *Vocal health and pedagogy: Vol. 1. Science and Assessment.* San Diego, CA: Plural Publishing.

Sundberg J. (1987) *The science of the singing voice* DeKalb, Il: Northern Illinois University Press.

Titze I.R. (2000) *Principles of voice production* Iowa City, IA: National Center for Voice and Speech.

Titze I.R. and Verdolini Abbott K. (2012) *Vocology; the Science and Practice of Voice Rehabilitation* Salt Lake City, UT: National Center for Voice & Speech.

Watson A.H.D. (2009) The biology of musical performance and performance-related injury. Lanham, MD: Scarecrow Press.

Welch G., Howard D. and Nix J. (eds.) (2019) *Oxford handbook of singing* Oxford: Oxford University Press.

About the Authors

Nicola Harrison, mezzo-soprano, is a passionate teacher of singing with a strong interest in all aspects of singing and performance from anatomy to artistry, and all that lies between. Her unique portfolio of skills in vocal, literary, medical, musical and pedagogical disciplines informs this book in many ways and her joint expertise as both a creative and an academic writer come together in this book, co-authored with Dr Alan Watson, and her third book written specifically for singers. With specialisms in anatomy, ENT and voice clinic following a degree in nursing, a second degree in English from University of Oxford and subsequent career as singer, performer and vocal pedagogue, her research into the vocal instrument, focusing on clarifying the language we use to teach singing and the use of imagery in accessing the muscles of vocal support has been presented nationally and internationally and is the subject of a future book on the singer's imagination. This research has included several years of collaborative work with Alan Watson as well as other projects involving three major universities, and a wide number of vocal experts and singers from several music colleges and conservatoires.

Her specialism in poetry and music was fostered by a BA and MA in English Literature at Oxford University and has led to an extensive portfolio of original writing, with multiple shows of words, song and music arranged for small bands and ensembles, a touring company, and two published books of poetry. She is in demand as both a singer and performance poet, with a particular focus on the Spanish and English song repertoire.

She has written two books about poetry and music for singers – The Wordsmith's Guide: Poetry, Music and Imagination. For many years she wrote a personal column in The Singer and Classical Music Magazine about poetry and music and performance. As a former journalist she has also written for other music-related media such as British Music magazine, and a variety of newspapers, journals and radio on matters of words and music. She is currently Lecturer in Singing and Interpretation at Pembroke College Oxford, where she teaches singing with a strong focus on vocal anatomy and technique, and continues her writing and research. She has taught at other Oxford colleges and universities and teaches privately, runs vocal workshops and teaches academics in both speaking and singing. Previous students have won international prizes, scholarships and Olivier Awards. She was also involved in setting up the singing course at the Billy Elliot Academy in Leeds with Mary Hammond, where she also taught for several years. She holds certificates in Adult, Further and Higher Education and has a PGCE.

Nicola won a Major Award to Oxford University. She also won the prestigious Wolfson Prize from Westminster Hospital, and two further scholarships, one of them to study singing with Pamela Bowden with whom she studied classical singing. She continued her vocal studies with the acclaimed vocal pedagogue and mentor, Pam Cook, MBE (RNCM), and subsequently with the legendary Spanish mezzo-soprano Teresa Berganza in Madrid.

Alan Watson is a reader in anatomy and neuroscience at the School of Biosciences, Cardiff University and has a lifelong interest in music. He plays the flute and French horn and has an interest in musical instrument construction. He took a B.Sc. in Zoology at Edinburgh University followed by a Ph.D. in Neuroscience from St. Andrews University and postdoctoral research at Cambridge University. He teaches anatomy and neuroscience to medical and science students and carries out research in neuroscience  and physiology on which he has published extensively. As recently as August 2019, he was awarded an Honorary Fellowship of the Royal Welsh College of Music and Drama (RWCMD) where he runs a module on the biological principles underlying musical performance and works with staff and students on projects dealing with performance physiology. He has collaborated over many years with Nicola Harrison on patterns of respiratory and abdominal muscle 'support' activity in singers. His other research involves brass players and deals with respiratory physiology, posture and embouchure function. This work has received public engagement funding from the Wellcome Trust. He is currently involved in a multi-conservatoire research project (Musical Impact) funded by the Arts and Humanities Research Council.

Alan lectures widely on the musicians' health and performance physiology at UK conservatoires and at science and arts festivals. This has included presentations on the science of singing and on breathing in singers for the BVA, AOTOS, the Three Choirs Festival, the Hay Festival and the Cheltenham Music Festival, and he has given lectures on singing-related anatomy and on breathing for courses for singers and voice therapists. He frequently lectures for clinicians at the British Association of Performing Arts Medicine and has had a long association with an M.Sc. degree course on Performing Arts Medicine at University

College London. His book on "The Biology of Musical Performance and Performance-related Injury" was published by Scarecrow press in 2009. He recently produced a chapter on Breathing in Singers for the Oxford Handbook on Singing (G. Welch, D.M. Howard. [eds.]) and has contributed to forthcoming editions of The Musician's Hand (I. Winspur [ed.] and the Cambridge Encyclopaedia of Brass (Herbert, T., Wallace, J., Myers, A. [eds.]) as well as publishing a number of papers on performance physiology. He is also interested in anatomical illustration and has provided his own figures for publications and books.

www.ingramcontent.com/pod-product-compliance
Lightning Source LLC
Chambersburg PA
CBHW080745250426
43671CB00038B/2873